Doing Less With Less

Making Britain More Secure

Paul Robinson

imprint-academic.com/societas

Published in the UK by Imprint Academic
PO Box 200, Exeter EX5 5YX, UK

Published in the USA by Imprint Academic
Philosophy Documentation Center
PO Box 7147, Charlottesville, VA 22906-7147, USA

ISBN 1 84540 042 9

A CIP catalogue record for this book is available from the
British Library and US Library of Congress

Contents

Preface

In constructing this book I have had to balance the need for brevity with the requirement to provide supporting data for the arguments I put forward. I have chosen to keep the main text short and to include much of the supporting material in the form of appendices. Readers who wish to know more about how I have reached my various conclusions are advised to refer to the relevant appendix.

I would like to thank Keith Sutherland of Imprint Academic for making the publication of this work possible. I am extremely grateful to him. I would also like to thank my military friends, and especially a certain lieutenant colonel, who have continued to stand by me despite my efforts to argue them out of a job.

About the Author

Dr Paul Robinson is Assistant Director of the Centre for Security Studies, and also Acting Director of the Institute of Applied Ethics, at the University of Hull, and is the author and editor of a variety of works on military history, military ethics, and international security. These include the books *The White Russian Army in Exile* (Oxford: OUP, 2002) and *Just War in Comparative Perspective* (Aldershot: Ashgate, 2003). He also writes regularly about international affairs for magazines and newspapers such as *The Spectator* and the Moscow-based newspaper *Rossiia*. He has served as an officer in both the British and Canadian armies.

Introduction

In the past decade, the government of the United Kingdom has embarked on an aggressive, interventionist military policy, which has seen the country's armed forces deployed overseas in ever-growing numbers, for ever-lengthening periods of time, and with an ever-increasing level of violence. From small-scale peacekeeping operations in the Balkans, to more forceful intervention in Sierra Leone and Kosovo, and most recently to all-out war in Iraq, the scale and tempo of operations has risen inexorably. At the same time, the manpower of the British armed forces has diminished, and will diminish still further following the government's statement on future defence capabilities issued in July 2004.[1] With increasing demands made on fewer people, the military are feeling stretched as never before. Unsurprisingly, critics of government defence policy are demanding that defence spending rise more rapidly to solve the growing crisis.

One should note, though, that if an organisation lacks the resources to properly carry out the tasks its leadership has set, more resources may not be the right solution. In the case of the armed forces, experience shows that the more capable they are, the more politicians demand of them. Additional resources rarely solve the problem. In the face of overstretch, cutting the number of tasks may be a better way forward. This book argues that this is in fact the case with respect to British defence policy. Military interventionism is neither necessary for Britain's defence, nor even beneficial to it. On the contrary, it undermines

[1] Ministry of Defence, *Delivering Security in a Changing World: Future Capabilities*, Defence Command Paper Cm 6269, July 2004 (London: The Stationery Office, 2004).

our security, and imposes undesirable costs on our nation. We should be doing less.

Doing less will not only enhance the security of the United Kingdom, it will also enable us to manage with less. The armed forces of Britain are now geared almost entirely towards interventionist expeditionary warfare. Rejecting that stance as contrary to our national interests will allow us to dispose of those military assets which are now wastefully being deployed in giving us the capability to wage such warfare. Disposing of these will allow us to spend less overall while also spending more on those aspects of security policy which are worthwhile – a double benefit which it would be foolish to reject.

We are now at a tipping point in defence policy. Ever since the collapse of the USSR, security experts, in an effort to defend their institutional interests, have been promoting the idea of military intervention – to meet the 'challenges' posed by 'failed states', 'rogue states', 'weapons of mass destruction', and so forth. A whole new vocabulary has developed to accompany this philosophy, including ideas such as 'peace enforcement', 'humanitarian intervention', and 'pre-emptive' (or 'preventive') war. Interventionism has become a dogma within defence circles, and among large sections of the political classes. It has now reached its logical conclusion in Iraq.

But the debacle of British policy in Iraq – the phantom 'weapons of mass destruction', the appalling intelligence failures, the shocking lack of planning for the post-war situation, the continuing resistance, and the boost given to Islamist terrorism by Anglo-American actions – has served to discredit the interventionist doctrine. It is becoming ever clearer that we cannot easily reshape the world for the better by the aggressive use of military force, and it is becoming obvious that efforts to do so, far from making us safer, serve only to harm us.

Barring an extraordinary reversal of his promise to retire before the next general election, Mr Blair's days as Prime Minister of the United Kingdom are now numbered. With his departure, an opportunity will come to abandon the policy of military intervention so closely associated with his premiership. To seize this opportunity, we need to start planning alternatives now.

The time has come, therefore, to challenge interventionism head-on, and to draw the necessary conclusions – that the creation of an increased capacity for expeditionary warfare has done us more harm than good, and that we would be better off in all respects if we were to dispense with this capacity as rapidly as possibly. The present book lays out this case. In so doing it hopes to begin a process which will produce a better defence policy for our nation – doing less with less, but doing it better as a result.

Part 1
British Defence Policy –
What It Is

Chapter 1

Military Intervention and Current Defence Policy

The British armed forces of today do not exist to defend the United Kingdom. That may seem startling, but it is the only logical conclusion to draw from the many documents issued by the Ministry of Defence over the past decade and from the actual activities which the armed forces have undertaken in that period. Whereas once our military existed to defend Britain and its interests, now its role is offensive and aggressive – to export by force a certain vision of what the world should be. The aim that government has set it is quite literally to be 'a force for good'.[1] The shape of the armed forces, their capabilities, and their methods of operating all reflect this concept. The core of British defence policy is now the doctrine of military intervention overseas. In practice, this policy has taken the form of armed attacks against Yugoslavia and Iraq. Now, further reforms are underway to enhance the capacity of our military to conduct further such attacks in the future. This is the reality of British defence policy. It is a policy not of defence, but of offence.

Over the past ten years, the government of the United Kingdom has gradually restructured the armed forces to enable them

[1]   Ministry of Defence, *Delivering Security in a Changing World*, Defence White Paper, December 2003 (London: The Stationery Office, 2003), p. 20.

to put the ideas of intervention into practice. These ideas have become the armed forces' *raison-d'être*. For this very reason, almost nobody within the defence community has seen fit to challenge whether the tasks associated with this concept are either suitable for the military, or even in the interests of the country. Interventionism has become what political scientists term a 'hard policy path', with a momentum of its own that makes it almost impossible to challenge from within the defence community. It therefore falls on those of us who stand outside that community to point out its flaws. The chief of these is that the basic assumptions upon which the policy is constructed are false.

Throughout their history, the primary role of the British armed forces has been to defend British territory – both the mainland of Britain and its overseas possessions – from attack by the armed forces of potential aggressors, be they Spaniards in the sixteenth century, Dutchmen in the seventeenth, French in the eighteenth and nineteenth, or Germans and Soviets in the twentieth. The collapse of the Soviet Union and the Warsaw Pact at the end of the 1980s put an end to all that. Suddenly, Western states, including the United Kingdom, found themselves unchallenged militarily. For the first time, wherever we looked there was no enemy capable of attacking us by conventional military means – not now and not in the foreseeable future.

The *Strategic Defence Review* (SDR) of 1998 recognised this new reality, stating clearly that 'there is no direct military threat to the United Kingdom or Western Europe. Nor do we foresee the re-emergence of such a threat'.[2] That Review hedged its bets, stating that it was still necessary to guard against the unlikely event of such a threat re-emerging. By 2003, though, the Ministry of Defence no longer considered even such a safeguard essential. The 2003 Defence White Paper thus commented that:

> It is now clear that we no longer need to retain a capability against the re-emergence of a direct conventional strategic threat to the United Kingdom or our allies. Priority must be given to meeting a wider range of expeditionary tasks, at greater range from the United

[2]   Ministry of Defence, *The Strategic Defence Review* (London: The Stationery Office, 1998), para. 3, p. 5.

Kingdom and with ever-increasing strategic, operational, and tacti-
cal tempo.[3]

This is a striking statement: not only is there no danger that
any other state will attack the UK, but the Ministry of Defence
believes that there is no danger of this happening at any time in
the future. There is, therefore, according to the ministry, no need
– none (it is worth repeating that: *none*) – for any armed forces,
any at all, to defend the UK against conventional attack. One
may argue that there is still a requirement for small numbers of
forces for counter-terrorist activities, assistance to the civil
power (as in the BSE crisis), search-and-rescue, and the like, but
the levels of expenditure required for that are far below those
currently envisioned.

In these circumstances, it is clear that the armed forces have
one primary purpose – the 'expeditionary tasks' mentioned earlier. Our military now quite openly exists primarily to project
British power overseas. In his introduction to the 'New Chapter'
of the Strategic Defence Review, published in 2002, the then Secretary of State for Defence, Geoff Hoon, spoke of the 'emphasis
on expeditionary operations', and of rapidly deploying 'significant, credible forces overseas. It is much better to engage our
enemies in their backyard than ours, at a time and a place of our
choosing and not theirs'.[4] (Since the MOD admits that nobody
can strike the UK by conventional means, one must suppose that
the enemies in question are 'asymmetrical threats' who intend to
attack us by non-conventional means, such as terrorism). In line
with this thinking, the 'New Chapter' made it clear that the tasks
of the armed forces are no longer simply deterrence, and if necessary defence against attack, but also include 'coercion',[5] a
remarkable addition which makes it clear how far Britain's
Labour government has redefined the concept of 'defence'.

The purpose of this expeditionary zeal is, at least in official
rhetoric, two-fold: first to shape the world for the better – to 'do
good'; and second, to crush enemies who lurk overseas before

---

[3]   Ministry of Defence, *Delivering Security in a Changing World*, para. 4.9, p. 11.
[4]   Ministry of Defence, *The Strategic Defence Review: A New Chapter* (London:
      The Stationery Office, 2002), pp. 4–5.
[5]   Ibid., pp. 9–10.

they have a chance to strike us here. One can see NATO's aerial assault on Yugoslavia in 1999 as an example of the former, and the invasion of Iraq as an example of the latter. Acquiring and maintaining the ability to launch such 'humanitarian interventions' and 'pre-emptive' wars is thus what defence planners are seeking to do.

In this regard, it is noticeable that the idea of projecting power did not originally seem to mean aggressive military action. The SDR spoke merely in terms of the need 'to help prevent or shape crises further away and, if necessary, to deploy military forces rapidly before they get out of hand'.[6] This could imply fairly benign activities, such as defence diplomacy, peacekeeping operations, or preventative deployments, such as that undertaken by NATO in Macedonia. However, the attacks on Yugoslavia and Iraq have put the focus back on offensive war. The 2003 White Paper and the defence statement of July 2004 make it clear that, pushed by financial constraints, the Ministry of Defence is sacrificing its ability to carry out operations such as traditional peacekeeping and conflict prevention (for instance, by cutting the number of infantry battalions), in order to finance the aircraft carriers and 'network-centric' equipment (airborne stand-off radars, etc) it needs to continue to carry out aggressive military activities against foreign states. As Timothy Garden and David Ramsbotham have pointed out, the 2003 White Paper made it clear that 'future defence priorities will be shaped primarily by the need to work with the US at the high-intensity end of the operational spectrum',[7]– i.e., the British armed forces are being reshaped specifically to engage in actions such as the recent invasion of Iraq, at the expense of alternative postures (for details of the order of battle of the UK armed forces before and after the July 2004 review, see Appendix 1).

The new structure of the armed forces reflects this new, offensive, often 'coercive', expeditionary role. The Royal Navy, for instance, has largely abandoned its traditional roles in favour of becoming a corral of floating weapons platforms for attacking

[6]   Ministry of Defence, *The Strategic Defence Review*, para. 77, p. 21.
[7]   Timothy Garden and David Ramsbotham, 'About Face: The British Armed Forces – Which Way to Turn?', *RUSI Journal*, April 2004, p. 13.

land-based targets far from the UK. This can be seen in the decision to acquire two new aircraft carriers, able to carry significantly more aircraft than those currently in service. One can also see the new priorities at work in the submarine fleet, as hunting other submarines slides down the order of importance, and our submarines instead act primarily as underwater cruise missile launchers. On top of this, the acquisition of new assault ships for the Royal Marines further adds to the ability to strike at other countries far from the UK.

The army, similarly, has changed its posture. The heavily armed and armoured divisions which sat in Germany during the Cold War are now almost entirely a thing of the past (1 (UK) Armoured Division, in whose headquarters the author of this book once served, is the sole exception – and even it is to be cut in size). They were too immobile to be easily deployed overseas. Transporting the hundreds of tanks, artillery pieces, trucks, and so forth which such divisions possess, requires a degree of logistical support which makes the worldwide deployment of large numbers of these forces impractical for any country other than the United States. Getting rid of the armoured divisions has meant fewer main battle tanks and less mechanised infantry and heavy artillery, but in their place have come more airmobile infantry and helicopters. To carry the new forces, the RAF is boosting its long-range transport capabilities.

When the government announced the latest plans to restructure the armed forces along these lines, there were inevitable complaints that the military had been 'stabbed in the back' because some units were destined to be cut (most notably four infantry regiments). But in fact, defence spending has risen consistently while Labour has been in power and the headline cuts disguise the fact that what is taking place is not force reduction but restructuring. This will indeed mean fewer of certain sorts of units, but at the same time it will mean considerably more forces of the sort needed to engage in expeditionary warfare. British forces will be increasingly able to deploy far from home, in larger numbers and greater speed, than ever before. That in essence is the logic of current British defence policy.

Chapter 2

Intervention: Choice or Necessity?

The last chapter made it clear that British defence policy is now based around military intervention overseas. The question which then arises is whether the UK has gone into the intervention business with such enthusiasm because it is required for the defence and security of the UK, or whether some other motives lie behind the decision. In short, is intervention a matter of choice, or necessity? If it is the former, then we can dispense with it without cost to our security.

The 2003 Defence White Paper identified three 'visions' for Britain's armed forces. These were:

- Defending the United Kingdom and its interests.
- Strengthening international peace and security.
- [Being] A force for good in the world.[1]

The second of these is superfluous. Either 'strengthening international peace and security' is one of the interests of the United Kingdom, in which case it belongs in the first category; or it is not, in which case we are concerned with it solely out of a desire to 'do good' – in which case it belongs in the third category.

In effect, therefore, defence policy as envisioned by the Blair government has two purposes – defence of the UK and transforming the world for the better. The first is unsurprising – it is what defence policy always has been, and should be, about. The

---

[1]   Ministry of Defence, *Delivering Security in a Changing World*, p. 20.

second is a startling new concept. It redefines the entire purpose of the British armed forces.

Being a 'force for good' is a proposition which has no place in a defence planning document. In the first place, it is entirely unnecessary. After all, what is the alternative – being a 'force for bad'? Whose 'good' are we talking about? How is 'good' defined? In practice, the concept's purpose is to give moral gloss to the policy of armed intervention overseas. What being a 'force for good' actually means is all too often armed aggression, such as that undertaken against Iraq. The language also suggests a severe misunderstanding of the role of armed forces. Soldiers are not social workers. They fight, and kill. That is what they are trained to do. Doing 'good' is not an appropriate definition of their tasks.

It is, though, the definition that Britain's Labour government has pushed to the fore in recent years. 'Defence' as such has fallen into second place. A quick glance at the Ministry of Defence's website confirms this. Incredibly, the very first words one confronts on the 'Army Jobs: Army Life' recruiting page are 'The British Army is a force for good'. The site then goes on to stress the army's activities 'around the world'. Defending the UK barely gets a mention.[2] Similarly, the Labour Party's defence website, under the heading 'Our Approach', states immediately that 'Labour believes that Britain should act as a force for good in the world'.[3] (One wonders whether they think that Conservatives believe that Britain should act as a force for evil.)

The 'goodness' concept seems to have evolved over the past seven years from being something of an afterthought to being the central plank of the UK's defence policy. In the 1998 SDR, the phrase 'force for good' did appear, but at the very end of the document, without any great emphasis.[4] Kosovo, however, seems to have convinced Mr Blair that military force was an appropriate means for reshaping the world for the better. The 1999 Defence

---

[2]   'Army Jobs; Army Life', available online at:
        www.army.mod.uk/careers/army_life/what_is_the_army.html
[3]   'Defence', available online at:
        php.labour.org.uk/pda/policy_article.phtml?id=29
[4]   Ministry of Defence, *The Strategic Defence Review*, para. 201, p. 53.

White Paper elevated the concept to its first chapter under the heading 'Our Security Priorities'. Even then, being a 'force for good' was the last of the defence priorities listed.[5] By 2003, the idea had been promoted again, now becoming one of the defence 'visions'.

Whether 'doing good' is desirable will be discussed in Part 2. First comes the question whether this is a policy of choice or necessity. Clearly, it is the former. One can argue that we have moral responsibilities to help others, that it benefits us to do so, and even that force is an appropriate tool in this regard, but it is hard to present a case that one *has* to intervene in this way. Had the UK failed to attack Yugoslavia in 1999, it is not obvious how the security of the UK would have suffered. Indeed, one of the justifications used in the conflict was precisely that NATO's action was not based on self-interest. Similarly, we could have left Sierra Leone alone, and suffered no harm from that. These things are not things that we *have* to do.

This, therefore, leaves as a hard requirement only the other plank of defence policy – the defence of the UK and its interests. The question here, then, is whether military intervention overseas on the scale now envisioned by defence planners is strictly necessary for our security. Could we have dispensed, for instance, with attacking Iraq and still remained secure? Or were vital security interests at stake which made intervention essential?

The logic behind interventionism is roughly as follows: post-Cold War the world has become more unstable, and is a more dangerous place; crises produced by failing states may spill over borders and damage our interests; the UK, furthermore, has numerous enemies overseas, who if left alone will seek to attack us; we must, therefore, take the fight to them, and intervene in their countries to restore order, reduce instability, and pre-empt attacks upon us.

There are numerous faults in this reasoning. In the first place, the idea that the world is more unstable now than in the past,

---

[5]   Ministry of Defence, *Defence White Paper 1999*, chapter 1, para 2. Available online at: www.mod.uk/publications/whitepaper1999/chapter1.htm

although popular, is mistaken. It seems that people have incredibly short memories. The perception appears to be that Cold War rivalries kept a lid on conflicts, as the superpowers acted to ensure that the world never became too unstable. In fact, throughout the Cold War the complaint was the opposite – that superpower rivalries incited conflict and instability, through mechanisms such as proxy wars. During the past sixty years, there have been no shortage of wars, insurgencies, and the like – including the numerous conflicts in South-East Asia, Africa, and South America. Most of these have now come to an end. It is true that a number of bitter ethnic conflicts erupted in the death throes of the Cold War (in Yugoslavia and Nagorno-Karabakh, for instance), but ethnic conflict is nothing new. Furthermore, despite the visibility of these examples, the incidence of ethnic conflict worldwide actually fell in the 1990s.[6] This is also true of war more generally. Several surveys of international conflict using a variety of methodologies have shown that the incidence of war has declined in the past fifteen years (as indeed has the incidence of terrorism). The world is getting more peaceful. (For more on the surveys in question, see Appendix 2.)

Two events have, though, proved to be godsends for the doom-mongers. The first was the Iraqi invasion of Kuwait in 1990. This gave credence to the rhetoric of 'rogue states' and 'weapons of mass destruction' as terrible new threats to Western security. The next event was the horrific attack on America which took place on 11 September 2001. This highlighted a new threat from Islamist terrorism. Put all three of the above together to produce a 'nexus of rogue states, terrorists, and weapons of mass destruction' and you seem to have a devastating threat which requires urgent preventive military intervention.

The problem with this 'threat' is that it is grossly exaggerated. In the first place, the intent of 'rogue states' to attack the UK has never been demonstrated. For the past decade the USA, which invented the 'rogue state' concept, has given seven countries that appellation: Cuba, Pakistan, Libya, Iraq, Iran, North Korea,

---

[6]   Y. Sadowski, 'Ethnic Conflict', *Foreign Policy*, no. 111, Summer 1998, pp. 12-23.

and Syria. Of these, the first, Cuba, is on the list purely for domestic political reasons and poses no threat to anybody; the second, Pakistan, is now America's ally; the third, Libya, has come in from the cold (indeed, Mr Blair has described its leader, Colonel Gaddafi, as 'courageous'); and the fourth, Iraq, is now under our control. So, the entire 'rogue state' threat comes down to three rather weak nations, none of whom could have any possible reason for launching an unprovoked, and surely suicidal, attack on the United Kingdom, and none of whom has the slightest capability of doing so even if, for some inexplicable reason, they did wish to. In short, the 'rogue state threat' is hardly a threat at all (and compared with the old Soviet threat, it is so miniscule and unimportant that it is a wonder that anybody takes it seriously).

Second, the hype about 'weapons of mass destruction' (WMD), and indeed the very phrase 'WMD', mask the fact that most 'WMD' are nothing of the sort. Nuclear weapons are certainly capable of mass destruction, but it is a terrible error of categorisation to place chemical and biological weapons (CW and BW) beside them. CW and BW are comparatively poor weapons, which it is extremely difficult to disseminate in a way which would cause mass destruction (this is especially true of BW). The main role of such weapons is to disrupt rather than kill – to close down areas for long periods while they are decontaminated. Certainly, if a terrorist acquired viable CW or BW, he or she could cause a huge amount of chaos and expense. But the loss of life would probably be small. One can kill large numbers far more effectively by packing fertiliser in a truck and blowing it up, as shown in Northern Ireland and Oklahoma (for more detail on WMD, see Appendix 3).

Third, the idea has become prevalent that terrorism now poses an 'existential threat' to the West. Mr Blair, for instance, has said that we are 'in mortal danger' and that 'the nature of the global threat we face in Britain and round the world is real and existential'.[7] This is bizarre. However much power terrorists have, they

---

[7]   'Blair Terror Speech in Full', BBC News, 5 March 2004. Available online at: news.bbc.co.uk/1/hi/uk_politics/3536131.stm

certainly cannot destroy Western civilisation or our way of life (unless we do it for them by over-reacting and destroying it ourselves). The threat from terrorism is one to individual lives, but not to our collective existence. Since 11 September 2001 a much-reduced risk tolerance has prevailed. One can observe this in Mr Blair's justification of the invasion of Iraq: 'do we want to take the risk? ... This is not a time to err on the side of caution.'[8] But Iraq precisely illustrates the fallacy of Blair's philosophy. One can make an argument that invading Iraq brought some benefits (especially to Iraqis), but the idea that we *had* to invade Iraq is nonsense. The threat from Iraq to the UK was zero. It had no WMD, no links with al-Qaeda, no meaningful offensive military capability, and no intent to attack the UK. If we had erred more 'on the side of caution', no harm would have come to Britain as a result. Instead, nigh on 100 British citizens (including 90 soldiers) have lost their lives, over two thousand have been wounded, our international reputation has been damaged, and we have boosted the cause of Islamist terrorism.

The philosophy of military intervention to tackle imaginary threats from overseas is not merely unnecessary, but actually harmful to our interests. Dispensing with this policy will not bring terrible consequences to our national security. Why, then has it taken hold of the military establishment so thoroughly? Three reasons stand out.

The first reason for military intervention is the existence of a capability to intervene, and the lack of constraints against it. We intervene because we can, and because nobody can stop us. The temptation to deploy military forces in support of diplomacy is too great, and having started down the military road, we find ourselves unable to stop ourselves going the whole way. As Major General Ian Durie, until 1996 Director of the Royal Artillery, noted in early 2003: 'There is a rush to war and, as those of us who are military men know, such large-scale troop deployments carry with them an almost inevitable need to use them'.[9] The speed with which the UK and USA adopted the new inter-

---

[8]   Ibid.
[9]   Obituary, Maj-Gen the Rev Ian Durie, *The Independent*, 18 May 2005.

ventionism once the restraining hand of the USSR had vanished
suggests that this is a prime factor. Confederate General Robert
E. Lee once remarked that 'It is well war is so terrible, else we
shall grow too fond of it'.[10] Western military superiority has
made war too easy, with exactly the consequence of which Lee
warned.

The second reason is bureaucratic. The end of the Cold War
deprived the military establishment of its *raison-d'être*. Interventionism is in favour for the simple reason that it is the only way
that existing institutions can survive and continue to justify their
budgets. One can see this logic clearly at work in NATO, which
is now obsessed with the policy of 'transformation', which
means restructuring NATO's armed forces to operate 'out of
area' – i.e. other than in defence of NATO territory. Former
NATO Secretary General Lord Robertson championed this policy, sloganeering: 'Out of area, or out of business'![11] The logic of
bureaucratic self-interest could not be clearer – the noble lord
did not, after all, say 'out of area, because our security demands
it', but in effect 'out of area, or our cosy institution will collapse'.
We shall see more logic of this sort at work in the European Security and Defence Policy in Part 3.

The third reason is blame avoidance by politicians. Especially
after the events of 11 September 2001, democratic politicians
have become very fearful of being held accountable should some
terrible 9/11-style disaster happen again. They have therefore
chosen to transfer the risk onto others. The calculation appears
to be that if, for instance, Iraq had weapons of mass destruction
and gave them to terrorists who used them against the UK, they
as politicians would be held to blame for doing nothing to stop
this. If, however, they invaded Iraq to prevent this and then discovered that there were in fact no weapons, people (indeed
many people) would be killed, but at least these would not be
Britons, and so the blame for the mistake would be compara-

---

[10] Douglas Southall Freeman, *Lee*, abridged by Richard Harwell (New York:
      Collier, 1961), p. 278.

[11] See for instance, a quotation from Robertson in 'The US and NATO: a
      Partnership in Action', US Department of State, available online at:
      usinfo.state.gov/is/Archive/2004/Jun/11-227891.html

tively light. From the politicians' point of view, the latter course seemed the safer. In essence, our leaders have engaged in aggressive war in order to cover their backs and preserve their reputations (with mixed success, as Mr Blair has discovered!).

This analysis makes it clear that interventionism has many roots, but none of them relate successfully to the actual security requirements of the UK. Institutional self-protection, intervening simply because one can, and the desire to be a 'force for good', are not necessary for our security. Nobody has adequately shown that if we eliminated our interventionist capability, our security would suffer as a result. To return to our original question, interventionism is a matter of choice, not of necessity.

Part 2
British Defence Policy –
What Is Wrong With It

Chapter 3

Philosophical Objections

Part 1 showed that current British defence policy centres around the concept of military intervention. It also showed that this policy is one of choice, not of necessity. But something may not be necessary while nonetheless being desirable. Part 2, therefore, will now argue that interventionism is not merely unnecessary, but also conceptually undesirable. This chapter outlines philosophical objections to the policy; chapter 4 outlines practical objections; and chapter 5 examines its costs.

In recent years, the number of euphemisms for war seems to have grown extraordinarily. Western states now engage in peacemaking, peace enforcement, police actions, humanitarian interventions, and 'operations other than war'. Of course, most of these 'operations other than war' are nothing of the sort. The coy words fail to disguise the true nature of these activities, which is that they are violent and coercive, and are war in all but name. What we are dealing with here is an effort to re-legitimise the waging of war, to make it once again an acceptable tool of foreign policy. Seen in that light, the policy of intervention confronts a whole range of philosophical objections.

Nearly everybody, one may assume, wishes to 'do good'. The ends are not in question. It is the means which are at issue; and as Mahatma Gandhi said, 'The means are the ends in the making'.[1]

---

[1]   Mahatma Gandhi, cited in Nigel Dower, 'Violent Humanitarianism – An Oxymoron?', in Alexander Moseley & Richard Norman (eds), *Human Rights and Military Intervention* (Aldershot, 2002), p. 77.

One does not have to be a devotee of Gandhi to accept that there is some truth in this. Even a devoted consequentialist, who believes one must judge an act solely by its outcome, must surely admit that if certain means consistently produce negative outcomes, there must be a strong case for establishing an absolute rule prohibiting those methods. To a large extent, the ethical objection to military interventionism rests on the grounds that war (for that is what it is) is an inappropriate tool for the conduct of foreign policy, and for 'doing good'. It is not a tool which we should be seeking to legitimise.

The Western world has a well developed set of criteria, in the form of 'just war theory', to determine in what circumstances force constitutes 'just' means. The central three criteria listed by Thomas Aquinas state that there must be a 'just cause', the war must be waged by a 'legitimate authority', and those waging it must have a 'right intention'.[2] Concepts such as humanitarian intervention immediately run up against objections on all three of these criteria. (Since Aquinas' time, more criteria have been added to the three listed here, but these remain a useful base for discussions of this sort – for further details and more analysis, see Appendix 4.)

In the first place, while mediaeval philosophers defined 'just cause' in terms of righting wrongs and punishing the guilty, in more recent times mankind has redefined it purely in terms of self-defence. One may fight justly if attacked, but not in other circumstances. This philosophical shift is not the result of some arbitrary decision, but the product of centuries of experience. Simply put, everybody claims to be on the side of justice. If acting on the side of justice constitutes 'just cause', then anybody has cause to fight at any time. Such a definition does nothing to restrain war, but rather facilitates it, by making it too easy to justify. It is open to too much abuse. If we claim a right to attack others in order to enforce western-defined 'human rights', it is all too easy for others to claim an equal right to wage war to enforce their version of morality.

---

[2]   Thomas Aquinas, *Summa Theologica*, vol. 2, part 2, question 40, 1st article (New York: Benziger Brothers, 1947), pp. 1359-60.

It is not for nothing, therefore, that in the twentieth century numerous international agreements, conventions, and treaties stated in the clearest terms that the only just cause for war was self-defence. This was made clear in the Charter of the United Nations, in several resolutions of the UN General Assembly,[3] and at the Nuremburg Tribunals. After the latter, German generals were hanged for committing the crime of 'waging aggressive war', a crime which was described by the American prosecutor, Justice Robert Jackson, as the 'most serious of all war crimes', because all the crimes of war derive from the initial decision to wage war. Yet 'waging aggressive war' – that 'most serious of all war crimes' – is precisely what Prime Minister Blair has done. Human rights abuses have been consistently rejected as a just cause, and until the Kosovo conflict the entire idea of humanitarian intervention was considered 'obsolete' for just that reason.[4] The International Court of Justice has pointed out that the 'right of intervention' is a 'manifestation of a policy of force, such as has, in the past, given rise to the most serious abuses'.[5] Yet, now, simply because it suits us to do so, we are discarding centuries of painful experience and the knowledge that it has given us regarding just causes for war.

Military intervention also runs into problems regarding legitimate authority. Neither NATO's 1999 campaign against Yugoslavia nor the Anglo-American invasion of Iraq had clear authority. Neither received the backing of the United Nations, and in both instances, large segments of the international community registered their opposition. This objection is not mere formalism. Legality matters. If one wishes to have any sort of international order, then it must be based on law, and obedience to the law thus acquires a moral imperative in and of itself. But more fundamentally, acts which lack legitimacy are a) morally doubtful, and b) likely to encounter opposition, which may ren-

---

[3]   For instance, resolution 2131 passed in 1965, and resolution 2625, passed in 1970.
[4]   Jarat Chopra, 'The Obsolescence of Intervention Under International Law', in Marianne Heiburg (ed.), *Subduing Sovereignty: Sovereignty and the Right to Intervene* (London, 1994), pp. 37-9.
[5]   Ibid.

der the activities fruitless. Furthermore, one must note that
much of international law and the institutions associated with it,
such as the United Nations, were creations of those states
(namely the USA and UK) which are now saying that they can be
ignored when inconvenient. Having created rules and institutions, and pledged ourselves and others to abide by them, it
behoves us to do so. As military analyst and former serviceman
Gwynne Dyer has noted, the UN is a 'cumbersome and meddle-
some monster' which nowadays 'nobody would dream of creating', but 'as a navy petty officer used to tell us many years ago
whenever he gave us the latest piece of unavoidable bad news:
"If you can't take a joke, you shouldn't have joined".'[6]

For all the talk of 'doing good', in practice this form of 'ethical
policy' takes the shape of attacking 'evildoers' rather than carry-
ing out positive acts of aid. This is an 'ethical policy of condem-
nation', a 'foreign policy of criticism',[7] which resorts to military
assault to remove those who have been criticised. But from
where does the UK's moral authority to act in this way derive? If
we act without the approval of the international community,
there is no clear answer to this question. Certainly, it does not
derive from the people on whose behalf we intervene. We neither ask their opinion beforehand, nor are accountable to them
post-facto. There is, as David Chandler points out, 'no mechanism to make the actions of the world's most powerful states
accountable to the citizens of the states in which they choose to
intervene'.[8] What redress do the citizens of Iraq or Yugoslavia
have against us? None, it appears.

The consequence of interventionist philosophy is, therefore,
to remove the constraints on the rich and powerful, without aid-
ing the weak in a corresponding manner. As the American academic Richard Falk has pointed out, the right to intervene is like
the Mississippi river; it flows in only one direction. We can inter-

---

[6]   Gwynne Dyer, *War* (New York: Stoddart, 1985), p. 258.
[7]   David Chandler, 'Rhetoric without Responsibility: The Attraction of
      "Ethical" Foreign Policy', *British Journal of Politics and International
      Relations*, vol. 5, no. 3, August 2003, p. 305.
[8]   Ibid, p. 307.

vene against the weak, but they have no commensurate power to intervene against us.

Finally, in terms of just war theory, interventionism fails because it is almost impossible to satisfy the criteria of 'right intention'. We may have maintained that our aim in Kosovo was to liberate the Kosovars, but may it not also have been to maintain the 'credibility of the NATO alliance', to stave off domestic political pressure 'to do something', or even to divert American voters' attention from Ms Lewinsky? Even the most benign-seeming of interventions may in truth be self-interested in intent, and thus immoral in fact (since moral philosophy recognises the vital importance of intention in the making of moral judgements).

Ethically, therefore, the entire thrust of modern British defence policy is problematic at best. Some commentators seem not to mind this, the American neo-conservatives being the most notable examples. For them, American values (and to these we may add British values, since they are not so very different) are so far superior to all others, that anything which spreads American (and similarly British) power is de facto a good thing, not only for America and Britain, but for everybody, whether they realise this or not. As Robert Kagan puts it, 'by advancing their own interests [Americans] advance the interests of humanity.'[9] America and its allies should therefore, according to one leading neo-conservative, William Kristol, be 'unapologetic, idealistic, assertive'. They should export their ways and values, and impose them on the world, for the good of the world. The neo-conservative agenda is unashamedly imperialistic. The end of the Cold War has, it is thought, brought an unprecedented opportunity. The West (most notably America) has a moment of dominant power, and it should use this moment for the good of all by promoting its interests determinedly and forcibly. Since this is for the good, not merely of the West, but of everybody, it should not let anyone or anything stand in its way in this holy task.

---

[9] Robert Kagan, *Paradise and Power: America and Europe in the New World Order* (London: Atlantic, 2003), p. 88.

Sadly, under the leadership of Mr Blair, the United Kingdom has been seduced by this dangerous philosophy. Blair at least has some excuse, since like the neo-conservatives he is an idealistic former man of the left, who has transferred his naïve youthful belief in the ability of socialism to reshape mankind into an equally naïve adult faith in the transformative powers of democracy. What is more surprising is the extent to which members of the Conservative Party have allied themselves to this line, to the extent of saying that they supported the war in Iraq even despite the lack of any Iraqi threat, because Saddam Hussein was a 'bad man'.[10] This attitude is perplexing because despite its name, there is nothing 'conservative' about neo-conservatism at all. It is a Trotskyite philosophy of permanent revolution, which believes in smashing existing institutions and structures in pursuit of some higher goal. The famous American judge Learned Hand once described a liberal as a man who thought he might be wrong. Conservatism is not dissimilar. It is based on a suspicion of grand ideas, and on a sense that drastic measures in support of abstract philosophy are unjustifiable because the philosophy is all too likely to be flawed. Such reasoning means that waging war to 'do good', ignoring international law, bypassing international institutions, and rejecting established definitions of justice, are all incompatible with both liberalism and conservatism. Those not standing on the extremist fringes of politics should give such policies short shrift.

---

[10] The Conservative Party's determination to continue raising defence spending is also somewhat surprising. Given the party's stated desire to cut taxes and root out wasteful government expenditure, one would have thought that defence represented an obvious target for cuts (especially since defence procurement contracts are famous for being massively over-budget). Yet for some reason, defence spending is a holy cow which is immune from all the normal criticisms of government waste. The reason is probably that Conservative MPs are mentally stuck in the Cold War period when high defence spending was a mantra which won them public support in the face of the Labour party's perceived weakness on defence. High defence spending has become an article of faith regardless of whether or not it is required.

Chapter 4

Practical Objections

Intentions and means are not the only criteria of moral philosophy. Consequences matter too. Hence, we should consider the actual consequences of military interventionism, the question being, 'does such intervention actually do good?' Experience suggests that, in fact, nine times out of ten, it does harm.

The simplest way to demonstrate this is to ask interventionists to list examples of successful disinterested military intervention (as opposed to traditional peacekeeping operations, which require the consent of all parties, and which have included both successes and failures). It is very hard to cite any, and certainly any successes are far outnumbered by the failures. The United States has invaded Haiti, for instance, on numerous occasions, most recently in 1994 – yet Haiti remains impoverished and politically chaotic (so much so that the United States actually encouraged President Aristide, whom it had intervened to help, to resign!). In Somalia, the international community fled with its tails between its legs, and the country remains a non-functioning 'failed state'; in Kosovo, inter-communal violence continues, the economy remains stagnant, and the province is rife with corruption and organised crime; and in Iraq, law and order seem almost entirely absent, the armed resistance continues to cause havoc, reconstruction has made little progress, and a city of 300,000 (Fallujah) has been destroyed and depopulated (at the time of writing, six months after the US attack on Fallujah, only 25% of its inhabitants have returned to their homes). If one wants one's military to be a 'force for good', experience suggests that the best method is to keep it as far away from foreign countries as possible.

Indeed, there is some evidence that the policy of intervention even encourages the sorts of human rights abuses it is supposed to eliminate. Some groups have realised that if they acquire victim status they may be able to persuade Western states to intervene on their behalf. Their leaders therefore incite attacks on their own community in order to achieve victimhood. This certainly happened in Kosovo. The Kosovo Liberation Army (classified as a terrorist organisation by the CIA) carried out regular attacks on Serbian civilians within Kosovo, killing and maiming innocent people in large numbers. The purpose of these acts was to incite a Serbian crackdown, which in due course would encourage NATO to intervene. In this way, NATO's professed willingness to step in and 'do good' in that region actually helped to provoke violent activity. Similarly, NATO's de facto annexation of Kosovo provided Albanian terrorists with a safe haven from which to attack Macedonia. When NATO leaders then pressed the Macedonian government to make concessions to the Albanians, the latter redoubled their efforts, hoping for a repeat of the 1999 events in Kosovo. NATO likes to portray its intervention in Macedonia as having ended the conflict there, but it was also partially responsible for starting it.

One may argue that in all these cases it was not the principle of military intervention which was at fault, but the manner in which it was conducted. Thus supporters of the invasion of Iraq like to claim that it was right to invade; it was merely the post-conflict planning which was defective. Such claims are false. Military force is an inherently unsuitable tool for 'doing good'. It is no accident that most interventions are failures; it is an inevitable product of their nature.[1]

Good strategy involves matching ends and means. In the military context, this means that one should direct force not towards

---

[1]   For a longer and more detailed exposition of the argument below see my earlier work: Paul Robinson, 'Humanitarian Intervention and the Logic of War', in Alexander Moseley & Richard Norman (eds.), *Human Rights and Military Intervention* (Aldershot: Ashgate, 2002).

'winning' in a purely military sense, but towards achieving the goal for which the war is being fought. This rarely happens. Once a war starts one cannot achieve one's political goals without overcoming the enemy. The latter, therefore, inevitably takes priority, even though, more often than not, the only way of overcoming the enemy is through the use of means which make it impossible to achieve the original political aim.

One may start a war for a clear objective, such as preventing a humanitarian catastrophe, but once it has started, that objective takes second place to achieving something called 'victory'. In effect, this means that humanitarian wars are humanitarian only until they begin. The moment they start they become simply wars, and the objective becomes winning the war, not fulfilling the humanitarian aims.

An awareness of this problem can help planners match ends to means more effectively, but there is good reason to believe that humanitarian interventions are even more prone to this mismatch than other military operations. This makes force a particularly poor tool for 'doing good'. The great military theorist Karl von Clausewitz provided a key to our understanding in this regard. He noted the tendency of military activity to move in a direction which contradicts political goals, and wrote:

> The more violent the excitement which precedes the War, ... so much the nearer will the military and political ends coincide ... but the weaker the motives and tensions, so much the less will the natural direction of the military element – that is force – be coincident with the direction which the political element indicates.[2]

The motives in humanitarian operations are weak ones – for the simple reason that they are not self-interested, and we are, therefore, willing to sacrifice less for them (as seen by the high priority given to 'force protection' in such operations). Ken Booth is thus right to conclude that 'Just wars encourage bad strategy'.[3] A prime example is NATO's bombing campaign against Yugoslavia. As the desire to protect the Kosovars was

---

[2]   Karl von Clausewitz, *On War*, ed. Anatol Rapaport (London: Penguin, 1982), pp. 119-20.

[3]   Ken Booth, 'Ten Flaws of Just Wars', in Ken Booth (ed.), *The Kosovo Tragedy: The Human Rights Dimensions* (London: Frank Cass, 2001), p. 317.

only a weak motive, NATO put a high priority on force protection and adopted a strategy of high-level aerial bombardment. This in the first place incited the very ethnic cleansing NATO claimed to be trying to stop (one must note here that nearly all the Kosovars who died in 1999 died *after* NATO began its attacks), and in the second place made it impossible for NATO to prevent the killing. As General Wesley Clark explained: 'You cannot stop paramilitary murder on the ground with airstrikes'.[4] Thus NATO's intervention made things worse. This was not simply a matter of mismanagement, it was a consequence of the nature of such interventions.

One can see the same process at work in Iraq. To 'do good' and help Iraq, coalition forces must restore order, and to do that they must defeat the insurgents. The desire to 'do good' is perforce subordinated to the desire to achieve military victory. In April and May 2004, this resulted in the ridiculous situation of so-called 'liberators' killing hundreds, perhaps even thousands, of those they were pledged to protect, in Fallujah and other cities of Iraq, and in November 2004 in the even more ridiculous situation of American forces actually destroying Fallujah (as was said in Vietnam, 'we had to destroy the village in order to save it'!).

In this regard, it is strange that the United Kingdom should have become so enamoured post-9/11 with seeking a military solution to terrorist problems. For the British armed forces have long been aware that military force is not the solution to terrorism. If we move the focus of attention away from 'doing good' and back to the simpler task of defending the UK against threats, we find that British military doctrine has for a long time stated that military interventions of the sort now being planned are not an appropriate response to the threats faced by the UK in the early 21st century.

British counter-terrorist and counter-insurgency doctrine is often said to date chiefly back to experiences in Malaya in the 1950s and the teachings of Robert Thompson, one of those responsible for the British success in defeating the communist

---

[4]   Wesley Clark, cited in Mary Kaldor, in 'Humanitarian Intervention: A Forum', *Nation*, vol. 270, no. 18, 8 May 2000, pp. 21-5.

insurgency there. Subsequent counter-insurgency experience in places such as Kenya and Oman, as well as counter-terrorist experience in Northern Ireland, has enabled the British armed forces to develop leading expertise and a sophisticated set of ideas for dealing with this kind of problem (see Appendix 5 for details). Our doctrine is directly contrary to the credo of aggressive military interventionism promoted by the United States (which has almost no counter-terrorist experience).

Simply put, until very recently British doctrine taught that terrorism is a political problem, which requires a political solution. The task of the military is to create conditions of stability in which that solution can be enacted. Because the focus of strategy is political, where military strategy conflicts with political strategy, the former must give way to the latter. Even if it makes military sense, for instance, to kill certain terrorists or enemy leaders, one should not do so if this undermines the political campaign by inflaming public opinion, encouraging more people to join the ranks of the terrorists, and so forth.[5]

So, faced by a problem of Islamist terrorism, doctrine should have dictated that the UK forge a political strategy to detach the terrorists from the bulk of the Arab population, and to remove the causes of discontent which incite Arabs to take up arms against us. Actions which inflame Muslim opinion should have been avoided. Yet what has Britain done? The exact opposite. However much Mr Blair may protest that the world is a safer place after the invasion of Iraq, the ever-increasing security measures being thrown up around public buildings in the UK indicate that those in authority feel that this is not the case. Indeed, CIA Director Porter Goss has admitted that the Iraq invasion has strengthened Islamist terrorists, telling the Senate Committee on Intelligence:

> Islamic extremists are exploiting the Iraq conflict to recruit new anti-US jihadists. ... These jihadists who survive will leave Iraq expe-

---

[5] The original outline of this doctrine can be found in Robert Thompson, *Defeating Communist Insurgency: Experiences from Malaya and Vietnam* (London: Chatto & Windus, 1967).

rienced and focused on acts of urban terrorism. They represent a potential pool of contacts to build transnational terrorist cells'.[6]

Military intervention is, therefore, not just ill-suited for humanitarian objectives, but also contrary to counter-terrorist doctrine and liable only to undermine our national interests, making us less, not more, secure. It is counter-productive. As one of Britain's most respected military officers, General Sir Michael Rose, has written:

> It is all too clear that the present strategy which is based on military intervention is not working – and that a radically different approach to global security is needed.[7]

---

[6] Porter Goss, cited in Dana Priest and Josh White, 'War Helps Recruit Terrorists, Hill Told', *Washington Post*, 17 February 2005, p. A1.

[7] Michael Rose, 'Change Attitudes, not Regimes', *International Herald Tribune*, 4 August 2004, p. 7.

Chapter 5

Costs

The costs of contemporary British defence policy are high. Of these, the financial costs are probably the least important. Defence spending is not so great that it is unsustainable, nor is it crippling the British economy. Nonetheless £34,000,000,000 or so a year is not an insignificant sum of money, and operations such as the invasion and occupation of Iraq do not come cheap (the cost for the UK of the war in Iraq so far has been several billion pounds; that for the USA over one hundred billion). If that expenditure is unnecessary and even counterproductive, there is an insurmountable case for reducing it. That said, other costs are more significant.

The first cost is in lives – 90 British servicemen dead in Iraq already, with more almost certainly to follow, dead in order to eliminate a threat to our security which did not even exist – lives pointlessly wasted.

The second and third costs are political and diplomatic – the damage done to Britain's prestige worldwide by the growing perception of our country as an aggressive military power, and the damage done to international institutions such as the United Nations, to the concept of international law, and to the idea of international society, all of which have served the UK well in the past.

The loss of prestige is especially important, as it badly damages the UK's 'soft power'. The distinction between 'hard power' and 'soft power' is one introduced by American thinker Joseph Nye, and is one which is often misunderstood. The difference between hard and soft power is not one between military force and gentler kinds of power. Rather, hard power is the power to make others do what you want when they do not want to; and soft power is the power to persuade them to want to do what you want. Hard power is coercive, soft power attractive.[1]

Soft power proved decisive in the Cold War. One of the dogmas of American Republicans is that Ronald Reagan brought down the Soviet Union through increased American defence spending. This is a myth. The USSR collapsed not because defence expenditure crippled it, but because its entire economy was faulty in design. Socialism did not work, and after 70 years this had become evident to all but the most hardened communists. They lost faith in their own system, which collapsed from within. And what made them realise that their ideology had failed was the evidence from outside – they could see that people in the West were richer and freer, and they wanted the same benefits for themselves. It was not our coercive powers that enabled us to defeat communism; it was our positive example, our soft power.

The potential for the West's soft power is enormous. Our economies are richer than those of other countries; our political systems are freer. There is every reason for people elsewhere to wish to emulate us. The European Union is an effective example of soft power at work. Non-members look at members, and wish to be like them. They then have to reform themselves to fit in the club – the EU thus changes them by making them want to change themselves. In the War on Terror, though, we have chosen to emphasise hard power. In doing so, we are abandoning our strongest card for one which is far weaker. We are giving people, especially in the Arab world, every reason not to emulate us, but to hate us. We are, as Nye points out, squandering our soft power with remarkable abandon.[2] We are becoming weaker as a result.

Interestingly, even some of the more fervent interventionists are slowly coming to realise this. For instance, Robert Cooper, a

[1]   See Joseph Nye, *Bound to Lead: The Changing Nature of American Power* (New York: Basic Books, 1990), for Nye's original explanation of soft power.

[2]   Joseph Nye outlines this argument is his latest book: *Soft Power: The Means to Success in World Politics* (New York: PublicAffairs, 2004).

former advisor on foreign affairs to Mr Blair, and a man sometimes cited as influencing the British Prime Minister in the direction of a form of liberal imperialist interventionism, once argued
that impending international chaos meant that 'Europeans need
to revert to the rougher methods of an earlier era – force, pre-
emptive attack, deception, whatever is necessary'.[3] More recently, however, he has somewhat changed his spots and warned
that 'military force has its uses, but running or transforming
other people's countries is not one of them'.[4] Spreading democracy is a good idea, he says, but not by force – 'in the end it is the
force of the idea and the power of its practice that conquers';[5] i.e.
it is soft power that ultimately prevails.

The damage done to soft power by the use of force shows us
that some of the greatest costs of our military policy are opportunity costs – in other words the costs we incur because by doing
one thing we lose the opportunity to do something else. Calcula-
tions of the profit and loss of certain policies all too rarely take
these into consideration, as they are hidden from view. But they
are no less important for that. Government is a limited good.
There are only so many things it can do. If leaders devote most of
their time to waging wars overseas, they will find that they have
insufficient time for other matters. This means that not only
domestic policy, but other aspects of foreign and security policy
suffer as a result. One of the saddest aspects of the many sad
aspects of the Iraq conflict is the way it has diverted government
attention from issues which are far more important, with dam-
aging consequences to our country's interests.

So, for instance, although Tony Blair has tried to show that he
has exerted influence on American policy by engaging the US in
the Israel–Palestine problem, in reality that problem has been
sorely neglected by all parties due to the huge time and effort
which has been spent on Iraq. This is somewhat bizarre, since we
claim that Islamist terrorism is our primary security concern.

---

[3] Robert Cooper, *The Breaking of Nations: Order and Chaos in the Twenty-First Century* (London: Atlantic, 2003), p. 62.
[4] Robert Cooper, 'Imperial Liberalism', *The National Interest*, no. 79, Spring 2005, p. 27.
[5] Ibid, p. 34.

The question of Iraq and its non-existent WMD was always irrelevant from the point of view of the 'Global War on Terror' (at least before we invaded – now, of course, we have turned Iraq into another breeding ground for terrorists). By contrast, the occupation of Palestine is of great significance in inciting Arab hatred of the West. The opportunity cost of invading Iraq has been the loss of opportunity to deal with this other issue. As American writer Morton Abramowitz points out, expressing a widely held opinion: 'Knowing what we now know about Iraq, one could make the argument that we would have been better off if we had spent only a fraction of the hundreds of billions our Iraq venture will end up costing us in bribing Arabs and Israelis into a settlement and enforcing it.'[6]

Abramowitz's statement draws attention to the fact that there are ways of solving problems other than force. The temptation to resort to expeditionary warfare detracts from these other methods, which are often more effective. If we really want to be 'a force for good', there are many ways of doing it other than attacking people, but there is little time or energy left for these ways once military action begins. Mr Blair once spoke of 'healing the scar of Africa', but has done noticeably little to put this idea into action (Blair's solution to such problems seems to be to form a committee or hold a meeting – in this case the Commission for Africa, and in the Palestinian-Israeli case the London Conference in March 2005. Activity resulting from such committees is scanty). If European leaders really wanted to help Africa and the Third World in general, the simplest and most cost-effective way of doing so might well be to scrap the European Union's Common Agricultural Policy, a move which would instantaneously boost the profitability of Third World agriculture. This would cost a fragment of what we spend on invading and occupying places such as Kosovo and Iraq, and bring far larger benefits, but it will not happen. Politically, it is too difficult.

Expeditionary warfare, by contrast, is comparatively easy – tell the forces to go and they go. Our armed forces have a

---

[6]   Morton Abramowitz, 'Does Iraq Matter?', *The National Interest*, Spring 2004, p. 44.

deserved reputation for efficiency and reliability. Ask them to invade somewhere, and they will, and they will do it well. This explains the attraction of military interventionism. It is an easy option, a quick fix, a way of appearing to act and be decisive. It is chosen because the resources are at hand, not because they are the best resources for the job, but once it is underway it blocks out all alternative options. Because of this, its cost is very great.

Part 3
British Defence Policy –
What Needs To Be Done

Chapter 6

Returning to Threat-Based Planning

We have now established that the focus of British defence policy
is military interventionism, that interventionism is not necessary for our defence, and that it is not even desirable, but actually
entails serious costs. This part of the pamphlet, therefore, moves
the argument on to determine what needs to be done to rectify
this faulty policy. Clearly, if we are spending our valuable
national resources on activities which are contrary to our interests, a review of that spending is necessary. This section begins
that review by urging a return to 'threat-based' defence planning, and from this draws the conclusion that Western states,
including the United Kingdom, already have sufficient capacity
for dealing with the threats to our national security.

One of the remarkable things about the defence world is the
prevalence of jargon and the speed with which it spreads, so that
once a new phrase appears, it is not long before almost everybody is repeating it as a God-given truth. Generally, the jargon
(often in the form of a TLA – three letter abbreviation) has a
shelf-life of about five years, after which something new comes
along. So, in the late 1990s, the prevailing buzz-phrase was 'Revolution in Military Affairs' (RMA); now it is 'Network-Enabled
Capability' (NEC); soon it will be something else. Often the purpose of the jargon appears to be to make something old appear to
be something new and trendy.

So it is with the terms 'capabilities-based planning' and 'effects-based warfare', both of which sound like wonderful new ideas, but are really statements of the blindingly obvious. Geoff Hoon explained the logic of these phrases in a recent speech to the House of Commons, in which he said that defence policy 'will see a shift away from an emphasis on numbers of platforms and people – the inputs which characterised defence planning in the past – to a new emphasis on effects and outcomes'[1] – ie one bases one's plans on the capability one wants, or the effects one wants to achieve, not on pure numbers of men and equipment.

This makes sense, but one wonders what the inventors of the jargon of 'capabilities-based planning' imagine planners did in the past – did they really base their plans on numbers alone, without *any* sense of what those numbers were meant to do? At the level of choosing what piece of equipment to purchase, capabilities-based planning is really no more than what planners have always done, but with a new name to make it appear that dramatic reform has taken place.

As far as that goes, it is harmless enough. However, the concept has caused serious harm when elevated from its origins in the process of defence procurement to the process of strategic defence planning. Now capabilities-based planning is how we are meant to organise our defence policy as a whole, replacing the 'outmoded' method of the past, known as 'threat-based planning'.[2] Because of this, defence planning has been turned upside down.

During the Cold War, in theory at least, the Ministry of Defence derived its policy from an examination of the threat (primarily, of course, the threat posed by the Soviet Union and its Warsaw Pact allies). Having determined what the threat was, planners then determined what we needed to deter, and if necessary, repel it. This was, therefore, 'threat-based' planning.

---

[1] Geoff Hoon, Speech to the House of Commons, 21 July 2004. Available online at:
news.mod.uk/news/press/news_press_notice.asp?newsItem_id=2958

[2] See the 2003 Defence White Paper, para 4.3., p. 10, for a specific statement to this effect.

When the Cold War came to an end, the 'threat' disappeared. If planning had continued along the same principles, its logical outcome would have been enormous reductions in defence expenditure. Probably for this very reason, at exactly the same time the Ministry of Defence discovered that a better method of planning existed – 'capabilities-based planning' – which fortuitously also happened to justify the maintenance of large defence budgets.

The new system works on the premise that you decide what capabilities you need, and then work out how to get them – what sort of systems you will need, what sort of financial resources, how many men, and so on. The problem with it is that it puts the end of the planning process at the beginning.

An examination of force planning models illustrates this point clearly. Such models give an indication of how force planners would like, in a perfect world, to go about their business, to produce a truly 'rational' product. In the real world, numerous factors (financial constraints, domestic politics, bureaucratic processes, etc) intervene and divert planning from the neat lines that the models show. But they remain a useful tool for evaluating the rationality of any given planning process. The closer the process to the model, the more sensible the process is; the farther away it is, the worse it is (for further details about force planning models, see Appendix 6).

Fundamentals of Force Planning, a guidebook produced by the US Naval War College, provides a number of such models, which in a much simplified form look roughly as shown in Figure 1 (overleaf.)[3]

Capabilities, one can see, are the final stage of this process. Capabilities-based planning is thus about as far from the model as one could possibly go, since it reverses the process entirely. Yet it is the concept on which a great deal of modern defence policy is built. The European Security and Defence Policy (ESDP) is a clear example. One might imagine that in working out what such a policy should be, European leaders would first determine

---

[3]   Adapted from diagrams in *Fundamentals of Force Planning*, vol. 1 (Newport, RI: Naval War College Press, 1990), pp. 107 & 150.

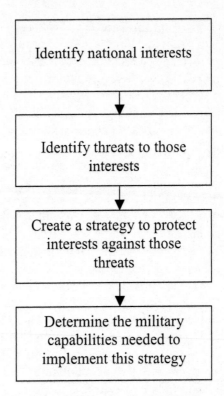

Figure 1: Force Planning Process

what the policy is meant to be securing and defending, then determine what they wish to do, and finally work out what resources they need to do it. On the contrary, almost the first step of the ESDP, long before it was clear exactly what the policy was for, was the establishment of a Capabilities Commitments Conference, which led to a Capabilities Catalogue, in which member states pledged certain resources for the use of the EU. The logic of the capabilities catalogue was that once European states had pledged certain resources, they would then feel bound to create them. The catalogue would thus force European states to increase their defence spending and strengthen their military capacity. As Geoff Hoon told the House of Commons, the ESDP is mainly 'a means of galvanising action ... a mechanism to improve European contributions to NATO'.[4] In other words, the entire process of ESDP is not at heart driven by security concerns, but by a desire to increase capacity as an end in itself. The approach seems to be to create the capabilities, and then decide what they are for. This is defence planning gone mad.

At this point, it is worth going back to basics, and reminding ourselves what the purpose of a security policy is. It is surely, above all else, to provide security. But that begs the question of how one defines 'security'. Simply put, security is 'freedom from threat'.[5] This definition makes it clear that security policy must relate to threats. How is it possible to determine what capabilities one needs, if one does not first consider against whom one might use them? The current philosophy of defence planning puts the cart before the horse. The only rational conclusion is that we should return at once to a system of threat-based planning.

The reason the defence establishment does not do this is, of course, that were it do so it would have to put most of itself out of business, because the threats to our security are small, and, as we have seen, military force is not an appropriate response to most of those threats which do exist. That reasoning should not, though, deter us from proposing such a course of action. Once we do so, we find that far from spending too little on defence, the UK, along with the rest of the Western world, spends quite sufficient.

According to the latest available statistics on world defence expenditures published in the International Institute for Strategic Studies' *Military Balance 2004-2005* (which actually only covers as far as 2003),[6] in 2003 the defence expenditure of the small club of NATO member states accounted for 62.8% of all global

[4] Geoff Hoon, 'Statement to the House on European Defence Co-operation', 22 November 2000. Available online at: news.mod.uk/news/press/news_press_notice.asp?newsItem_id=765

[5] For a list of various definitions of security, most along these lines, see Barry Buzan, *People, States and Fear: An Agenda for International Security in the Post-Cold War World* (London: Harvester Wheatsheaf, 1991), pp. 16-17.

[6] All figures in this section are calculated from statistics in *The Military Balance 2004-2005* (Oxford: OUP on behalf of the International Institute of Strategic Studies, 2005).

military spending. This percentage has undoubtedly grown since then, due to the large increases in US defence spending in the past two years, as well as the addition of several new members to NATO. Even the much-maligned Europe, which, we are constantly told, does not spend enough on defence, in fact spends a very great deal. The EU as a collective whole spent over $200,000 million in 2003 – almost twice the expenditure of Russia and China combined. EU members have over four million troops permanently under arms, plus another four million reservists (for more detail on international defence spending and force levels, see Appendix 7). Since the Ministry of Defence has stated categorically that there is no conventional military threat to us, nor is one envisioned in the future, we must conclude that this enormous expenditure is primarily to defend us against asymmetrical threats such as terrorists – i.e., eight million soldiers and 200 billion dollars to protect us from a few thousand men armed with nothing more sophisticated than Soviet-era rocket propelled grenades. The excess capacity is staggering.

Chapter 7

The Precautionary Principle

The case for eliminating some of this capacity thus seems overwhelming. At this point, though, proponents of such a policy run up against the precautionary principle, in other words the idea that it is better to keep spending high 'just in case' (for more details about the precautionary principle to supplement this chapter, see Appendix 8). Roughly speaking, the precautionary argument would go something like this:

> I agree with all the above, but the world is an uncertain place. One just doesn't know what lies around the corner. It is true that at present we don't need armed forces as large as those we have, and it is true that having them involves costs, but we can't be one hundred percent sure that we won't need them at some undetermined point in the future, and we have gotten our intelligence wrong before. Better to play safe, and keep what we have.

This argument has some strength. As pointed out earlier, any good liberal or conservative thinker should be aware of the possibility that he might be wrong, and should, therefore, avoid extreme actions on the basis of pure reason. If one took this book's arguments to extremes, one could use them as a basis for eliminating the armed forces almost entirely. But experience teaches us that the world does often take unexpected turns for the worse. There is some benefit in practising a bit of caution.

The precautionary principle is, though, a very weak one on which to hang an entire policy. It is also noticeable that people apply it inconsistently. So, for instance, the current US administration insisted on applying it in the case of Iraq (one couldn't be sure that Iraq had WMD, had links with al-Qaeda, or planned to attack the West, but *if* all three were simultaneously true, the dangers were so great that one couldn't take the risk); but the same administration is noticeably unwilling to apply it in other cases, as in, for instance, the case of global warming and the Kyoto agreement. This makes one think that something else lies behind the decision to refer to the precautionary principle, and that the principle itself is not the real determinant of action.

There are, after all, any number of things to worry about, and we cannot protect ourselves against them all. We have limited resources. So we use those resources to protect ourselves against those threats which we believe are most likely to occur, and which we can best defend ourselves against. In theory, for instance, little green men (LGMs) from outer space *might* attack Earth with weapons of extreme mass destruction, and kill us all. On 8 October 1955, General Douglas MacArthur told cadets at the US Military Academy West Point that 'the next war will be an interplanetary war. The nations of the earth must someday make a common front against attack by people from other planets'. But we are not taking MacArthur's advice, and exerting ourselves to create an interstellar defence system against the LGM threat. The reason is simple. We do not actually believe that such an event is at all likely. In other words, the mere possibility of something happening is insufficient grounds for protecting against it. Nobody protects themselves against everything. Nor can we be safe from everything. As Julian Morris has pointed out, 'all human activity involves risk, so the only way to achieve zero risk is to die'. 'If someone had evaluated the risk of fire right after it was invented', Morris says, 'they may well have decided to eat their food raw'.[1]

Besides, if one wishes to play safe, why not spend twice as much as at present, or three times? There has to be some logic beyond pure caution, or spending levels become entirely arbitrary. In short, 'just in case' is not an argument in and of itself. One has to provide some evidence that the case in question is

---

[1]　Julian Morris, *Rethinking Risk and the Precautionary Principle* (London: Institute of Economic Affairs, 2000).

likely and that protection against it is cost-effective. So, if one wishes to maintain high defence spending 'just in case', it is necessary to go beyond a mere feeling that something awful might happen sometime. One must produce some solid evidence about what it is that one fears, and prove that the risks involved in doing nothing outweigh the known costs of acting. Yet, as we have seen, the Ministry of Defence itself has admitted that not only is there no conventional threat to the UK at present, but there is no prospect at all of any such threat in the future, and it is no longer worth bothering with the possibility. Clearly the MOD itself does not believe in the precautionary principle.

Furthermore, the precautionary principle is not a cost-free option. It makes sense to follow it if no harm accrues from it – in such circumstances, there is no logic in not 'playing safe'. But the problem is that in the case of defence spending, harm inevitably does accrue.

We in the UK like to mock the motto of the American National Rifle Association: 'Guns don't kill people, people do'. We fully understand that the mere presence of guns makes it considerably more likely that people will use guns. If they are not there, people cannot use them. Yet somehow, we are unable to apply the same logic to military forces, and refuse to accept the premise that the mere existence of armed forces is a cause of armed conflict. But the evidence suggests that it is.

In the first place, international relations experts have long been aware of the so-called 'security dilemma'. To protect oneself from a threat, one builds weapons, but the presence of those weapons then threatens others, who in turn build more for themselves. Tensions mount, and insecurity increases. Paradoxically, it is often the case that the more one spends on security, the less secure one becomes.

Second, it has simply become too easy for Western states to use the military forces at their disposal, and so the temptation to do so has increased. If one keeps defence forces 'just in case', one will find oneself tempted to use them for something more practical than just sitting around expensively waiting for some unknown future cataclysm which may never happen. The mere existence of the forces will, therefore, lure one into the sorts of military interventions which this book has shown are so detrimental to our interests.

Robert Kagan illustrates this through a comparison with men wandering in a forest. A man without a gun will try and pretend that no bears exist or do his best to stay clear of any that might be there. But another man who has a gun will shoot on sight any bears he meets, just in case they are a danger, because he has no incentive not to play safe. America, Kagan says, is like a man who has a gun; Europe like a man without one. This explains the former's preference for military interventionism.[2] Kagan seems to think that the American way in this instance is a good thing. But the problem is that all too often the 'bears' turn out to be bunny rabbits or, in the case of Saddam Hussein's Iraq, bears who have lost all their claws and teeth and can barely move a foot beyond their lairs. However one looks at it, what Kagan is saying is that the mere ownership of military force encourages its use.

If anybody doubts that this happens in reality, they have only to turn to the words of former American Secretary of State Madeleine Albright. Pressing for NATO to attack Yugoslavia, Albright ran up against the opposition of the then Chairman of the Joint Chiefs of Staff, Colin Powell, who told her that this was an inappropriate use of the US armed forces. In reply, the Secretary of State asked Powell, 'What good are those forces if we can't use them?'

Albright's logic indicates that keeping armed forces in reserve on the precautionary principle invites abuse, for although the administration which creates those forces intends nothing more than to keep them to cover some unforeseen eventuality, a future government will eventually come to power which will want to *use* them.[3] And in the modern world, Western military power is

---

[2]   Kagan, op. cit., p. 31.

[3]   Seventeenth and eighteenth century British and American political thinkers such as John Locke were well aware of the dangers associated with powerful standing armies. See, for instance, John Trenchard's *Argument Shewing that a Standing Army is Inconsistent with a Free Government, and Absolutely Destructive to the Constitution of the English Monarchy* (London, 1697). Writing under the pseudonym *Cato*, Trenchard, along with Thomas Gordon, later argued that 'Standing armies are

so overwhelming, compared with that of any potential enemy, that there is precious little in practice to prevent it from doing so. As long as we have the capability to intervene militarily around the world, we will keep on intervening. The only way we can stop ourselves from engaging in this self-destructive activity is to deprive ourselves of the means of so doing.

standing curses in every country under the sun', describing them as 'the ready instruments of certain ruin' (*Cato's Letters*, nos. 94 & 95). This sentiment found reflection in the *Antifederalist Papers* opposing ratification of the US Constitution (see paper no. 28, 'The Use of Coercion by the New Government'). For some reason this traditional strand of Anglo-Saxon thought has been forgotten. It is time to resurrect it.

Chapter 8

The Way Ahead

Writing in *The Spectator* in June 2004, former Conservative Defence Secretary John Nott paraphrased in advance the logic of this pamphlet:

> One day we will no longer have an evangelist as Prime Minister and the passion for neo-imperialist do-goodery — joining with the Americans to bring democracy to Johnny Foreigner, pre-empting threats by taking war to the enemy as a subsidiary of the Pentagon — all of this will fall out of fashion. Someone will say that high-cost, high-technology warfare as a small reinforcement to the massive resources of the US is beyond our means; we should spend more on the police, the security services, the poor old British infantry and our reserve forces … The problem is that ministers are not in charge; the defence establishment has taken over.[1]

Nott is exactly right. In recent years, the defence establishment has successfully convinced the government of Mr Blair that it needs to create ever-more powerful expeditionary forces to act as a 'force for good' to bring order to a world which supposedly grows more dangerous by the day. In consequence, the United Kingdom has been sucked bit by bit into a series of overseas conflicts which have left many of our fine soldiers dead, but have brought little or no benefit to the security of the nation. It is time to bring this policy to an end, and to dismantle the military apparatus which goes with it.

What exactly this would mean in practice is dependent largely on the degree of caution one wishes to observe. As the last chapter made clear, caution is not a sufficient basis for maintaining everything that the British military now possesses, but

[1]   John Nott, 'Diary', *The Spectator*, 19 June 2004.

destroying everything would suggest an arrogant belief in the absolute correctness of our reasoning. Because of this, the suggestions for changes made below include both absolutist versions and more moderate options for those wanting to play a little safer.

Once one dispenses with expeditionary warfare, certain targets for reductions in the armed forces stand out clearly. The first are the Royal Navy's two new aircraft carriers, which are the centrepiece of the expeditionary armed forces.[2] Getting rid of the aircraft carriers, whose capacity is far above anything needed for purely defensive purposes, would save the British taxpayer up to £4 billion pounds. It would also liberate large sums to be spent on other parts of the defence budget (e.g. the infantry), which are now being sucked dry to pay for the aircraft carriers.[3] One could pocket these savings in full by not building anything in their place, or, if one wished to retain some power projection capability, perhaps accept a lesser option of a smaller aircraft carrier, along the lines of those already in service, or some small helicopter platform, which could be used for purposes such as the evacuation of British citizens trapped in conflict zones around the world. Such a capability would be justifiable even in a context which rejected interventionism, as evacuations of this sort are purely matters of the defence and protection of British subjects.

The submarine fleet would be another obvious target. In its July 2004 statement on future capabilities, the Ministry of Defence announced a reduction in the UK submarine fleet from eleven to eight by 2008. Since the primary purpose of the remaining eight now appears to be to act as underwater cruise missile launchers – an offensive role which the review proposed here would reject – one can make a good argument for eliminating

---

[2] I am very grateful to the naval expert Dr Eric Grove for his technical advice on matters concerned with the Royal Navy, though I wish to stress that the opinions expressed here are all mine.

[3] One should also note that the entire aircraft carrier programme seems to be running into severe problems (not itself an unusual phenomenon with large defence procurement projects), which means that its costs may well prove to be even higher than the £4 bn predicted above. This will have a deleterious effect on the rest of the defence budget, sucking even more money away from other projects.

them as well. More cautious planners who want to keep some submarine capability might like to keep them, and put them back to their original task of hunting other submarines to protect the surface fleet and our nuclear deterrent (though the submarine threat at present is low). Even if one pursues that option, the investment in the latest generation of Tomahawk land attack missiles should be cancelled.

Finally, as far as naval forces are concerned, an end to expeditionary warfare would raise serious question marks over the future of the two new amphibious vessels commissioned for the Royal Navy. One can certainly make a case for scrapping them both, or perhaps only one of them if one wishes to retain some capacity for 'non-combatant evacuation operations'. Memories of the Falklands War of 1982 will raise some eyebrows regarding the proposals above but, unlike in 1982, Britain now has the capacity to defend the Falklands against attack (due, for instance, to the building of better airport facilities), and no longer needs to rely on a strategy of re-capture.

The heavy investment in the aircraft carriers is currently forcing the Royal Navy to cut its investment in the surface fleet, with reductions in the numbers of destroyers, frigates, and minesweepers. The cuts proposed here would therefore have the advantage of allowing the Navy to invest better in that part of its inventory. There will always be a need to protect civilian shipping on the high seas, yet as a result of cuts in the surface fleet, the Navy will soon be dropping one of its six standing patrol commitments. We are, therefore, abandoning necessary tasks at sea in order to finance an unnecessary strategy of aggressive power projection against targets on land. This makes little sense, and the savings mentioned here will actually enable the Royal Navy to carry out its most important functions more effectively.

Cuts in the Army would also follow any abandonment of the interventionist philosophy. Already, the MOD is proposing to cut the Army's armoured brigades from three to two. One may doubt, given the lack of conventional threat to the UK, whether there is any need for heavy armoured forces at all. One could, therefore, argue for their entire elimination. As a lesser option, though, if one wished to maintain some knowledge base in the area of armoured warfare, one could instead just cut one brigade, to leave the Army with a single armoured brigade. This would suffice to provide a cadre of armour-trained personnel in the event that a requirement for it reappeared in the future.

Other arms would also be at risk. The Royal Artillery is a prime example. Already, the artillery is being restructured to reduce the numbers of heavy guns and to increase the numbers of lighter ones. This is part of the effort to make it more mobile, and so more deployable on expeditionary operations. Eliminate this requirement, and one could usefully dispense with much of the newer lighter artillery. In addition, the end of the interventionist strategy will eliminate the requirement for the huge volume of combat service support needed to maintain operations overseas. Big reductions in combat service support should thus be possible.

The main beneficiaries of such changes would be the infantry. It is one of the absurdities of current reforms that the infantry is being cut at a time when it has never been more in demand. Recent events in Iraq have shown that there is truly no substitute for boots on the ground, generally in a low-tech format. Whatever happens in the future, we will certainly always need a large force of basic infantrymen. Eliminating excess capacity of the sort mentioned above will allow the British Army to revive its infantry force.

The Royal Air Force will undoubtedly be the greatest victim of any reforms which dispose of expeditionary warfare. For a start, the cancellation of the aircraft carriers will eliminate the Joint Strike Fighters (JSF) which will fly from them, so depriving the RAF of one of the main planks of its future existence.[4] The other main plank is the Eurofighter (Typhoon). This is already an

[4] In fact, the development of the JSF is proving even more problematic than that of the aircraft carriers. Already the programme is two years behind schedule and the US Congress's Government Accountability Office has declared the JSF programme to be so complicated as to be 'unexecutable' (see 'Trouble for Joint Fighter', *DefenseTech.org*, online at: www.defensetech.org/archives/001515.html). There is a serious danger that the aircraft carrier/JSF project may turn into a massive white elephant, absorbing ever more funds but resulting in doubtful capabilities. Scrapping it will bring great benefits to other cash-strapped parts of the defence establishment.

obvious target, since it is a fighter plane designed to destroy enemy aircraft, but there is little discernible air threat to the UK at this time. As such, though, the Typhoon is a defensive machine and has some role in a strategy based on protecting the homeland. There will always be a basic requirement for some air defences, even if only to protect against a British version of the September 11th hijackings in the USA. Even in the current situation, many commentators are saying that the proposed Typhoon fleet of over 200 planes is excessive, and that 90 would suffice. A more extreme version of the strategy outlined in this book might go farther than that, but more cautious planners might wish to accept a figure of 90 as a reasonable compromise.

If the UK no longer seeks to export military power so ruthlessly overseas, the expanding airlift capacity of the RAF is also an obvious target. With reduced intervention forces in the Army available for airlift, some of this capacity would have to go. Altogether, therefore, the RAF appears to be extremely vulnerable on all fronts.

Parallel with these cuts, planners should consider increased investment in the reserves. The smaller the regular force becomes, the greater the reliance one should place on reserve forces to expand the military in time of crisis. In recent years, the reserves have suffered, with major cuts after the SDR of 1998. It is probably time to reverse these cuts, and our reserve forces should profit from a policy which renews the emphasis on defence of the United Kingdom.

Finally, the question of Britain's nuclear deterrent is one which must be considered. Press reports at the time of the 2005 British general election suggested that Prime Minister Blair had decided to begin the process of research and development to create a new deterrent to replace Trident 20 years or so from now (given the long lead times in such projects, planning must start soon if we are to maintain this capability). However, there has been almost no public discussion of whether this is advisable. Time and space preclude a detailed analysis of the question here, but one can certainly make a case that Britain no longer needs nuclear weapons. During the Cold War, when we desired a deterrent against the Soviet Union, such weapons made sense.

Now, it is much harder to see what purpose they serve. Eliminating the deterrent would allow us not only to scrap the Trident submarines but also the associated support facilities and those parts of the fleet which are dedicated to protecting them. The money saved could be used to bolster those parts of the armed forces which actually do serve a practical purpose and also to cut taxes or invest in other services.

Deciding exactly what should be cut, and what should be increased, is, however, a less important matter than establishing the basic principle that the policy of military interventionism is contrary to the interests of the United Kingdom, and that we should abandon both it and the paraphernalia of expeditionary warfare associated with it. Once that principle has been agreed, the rest will follow naturally.

The growing realisation of the faulty logic behind the Anglo-American invasion of Iraq gives us an opportunity to carry out the necessary re-evaluation, and to convince a future British government to avoid similar error in the future. We must seize this opportunity. If we do, we shall be more, not less, secure as a result.

Appendices

UK Armed Forces Order of Battle

The following table details those elements of the UK armed forces which will be cut over the next few years as a result of the July 2004 defence review.

Figure 2. Projected cuts in the UK armed forces

Royal Navy

3 Type 42 destroyers (out of a current total of 42)
3 Type 23 frigates (out of a current total of 16)
3 Submarines (out of a current total of 11)
3 Minehunters (out of a current total of 21)
1,500 personnel (out of a current total of 37,500)

Army

4 infantry battalions
7 tank squadrons (80-90 Challenger 2 main battle tanks)
6 artillery batteries (33 AS90 self-propelled guns)
96 anti-aircraft launchers
1,500 personnel (out of a current total of 103,500)

Royal Air Force

3 squadrons of Jaguar strike aircraft
1 squadron of Tornado fighter aircraft
The RAF Regiment
5 Nimrod maritime patrol aircraft
7,500 personnel (out of a current total of 48,500)

Superficially, these appear to be major cuts. However, one must bear in mind that the armed forces will also be receiving substantial quantities of new equipment to reinforce their expeditionary role. These include two new aircraft carriers, whose capacity is far greater than those currently in operation; eight Type 45 destroyers; the new Astute class submarines; some 200 Typhoon fighter aircraft; 150 Joint Strike Fighters; more heavy lift capacity; more light armour and reconnaissance forces; and increases to the special forces. At the end of the restructuring process the armed forces will have fewer people and fewer weapon platforms, but a greater strike capability (the newer equipment being more powerful) and an increased capacity to carry out military intervention overseas.

Incidence of War and Terrorism

An important part of the argument in favour of high defence spending and the doctrine of expeditionary warfare is the idea that the world has become more dangerous and unstable since the end of the Cold War. Those who believe this say that new threats, most notably terrorism, have arisen to replace those of the past and require a pro-active, interventionist response. Furthermore, they claim, the nature of war has changed, 'new wars' being particularly brutal and anarchic compared with traditional 'old wars'. Chapter 2 pointed out that these claims are false. This appendix provides further detailed data to justify that rebuttal. As is clear from the evidence below, there is less conflict and instability now than during the Cold War, terrorism is declining, and 'new' wars are not any worse than 'old' ones (indeed the distinction itself is false).

One caveat is necessary at this point. Assembling data on war and terrorism is complicated because much depends on how one defines a 'war' or a terrorist incident. Different surveys use different definitions, and consequently produce slightly different results. The US State Department, for instance, measures only 'significant terrorist incidents' and does not include in its survey of terrorist acts any attacks on military forces. This excludes, for instance, attacks such as those which used to be undertaken by the IRA against the British Army and those now being carried out by insurgents in Iraq against American forces. Yet some analysts consider these to be 'terrorist' actions, and one might also wonder why only 'significant' incidents are measured since failed attacks and incidents which result in only a few casualties are also meaningful. Such considerations mean that one can only draw sound conclusions about the incidence of such events by cross-referencing several different surveys which use a variety of methodologies. This is the approach I have adopted below. What is striking is that whatever methodology is used, every survey finds that the incidence of both war and terrorism has declined over the past 15 years.

The Declining Incidence of War

In an article in the journal *Security Dialogue* in June 2004, Edward Newman noted that, 'the incidence of both interstate and civil war has shown a marked decline since the early 1990s'.[1] Newman's opinion is confirmed in detail by reports from the Canadian group Project Ploughshares and the Stockholm International Peace Research Institute (SIPRI). According to the former's *Armed Conflicts Report 2004*:

> In 2003 the number of armed conflicts totalled 36 in 28 countries. These numbers are a slight decline from 2002 which saw 37 armed conflicts in 29 countries. The drop continues a general downward trend since a peak of 44 conflicts in 1995 and involves *the fewest number of states hosting wars since Project Ploughshares began tracking armed conflict in 1987* [emphasis added].[2]

SIPRI's figures are somewhat different as it counts only those conflicts involving 1,000 battlefield deaths in a given year. Nonetheless, SIPRI perceives the same decline, saying that, 'In 2003 there were 19 major armed conflicts in 18 locations, the lowest number for the post-Cold War period with the exception of 1997, when 18 such conflicts were registered.' It charts the number of 'major armed conflicts' between 1990 and 2003 as follows:[3]

---

[1]　Edward Newman, 'The "New Wars" Debate: A Historical Perspective is Needed', *Security Dialogue*, vol. 35, no. 2, June 2004, p. 180.

[2]　Project Ploughshares, 'Introduction', *Armed Conflicts Report 2004*. Available online at: www.ploughshares.ca/content/ACR/ACR00/ACR04-Introduction.html

[3]　Chart (figure 3) made by the author using data in Appendix 3A, *SIPRI Yearbook 2004: Armaments, Disarmament and International Security* (Oxford: OUP, 2004), p. 134.

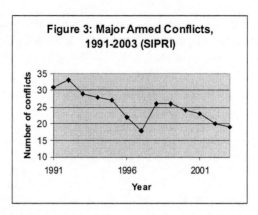

Figure 3: Major Armed Conflicts, 1991-2003 (SIPRI)

The temporary rise in the late 1990s was due to an upsurge of conflict in Africa, while the situation was stable elsewhere. The chart as a whole, though, confirms a downward trend in armed conflict in the 1990s and early 2000s.

Another, earlier, analysis[4] of the incidence of war in the 1990s, using a broader definition of war than SIPRI's, came to similar conclusions – a sharp rise in wars in the early 1990s followed by a sharp decline since 1992:

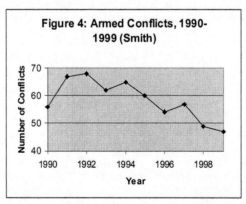

Figure 4: Armed Conflicts, 1990-1999 (Smith)

A fourth survey, which uses yet another methodology (counting all conflicts causing 25 or more battlefield deaths per year) was undertaken by the Conflict Data Project in the Department of Peace and Conflict Research at Uppsala University, and pub-

[4]   Dan Smith, *Trends and Causes of Armed Conflict*, Berghof Research Center for Constructive Conflict Management, www.berghof-handbook.net

lished in 2002. Its conclusion is that, 'The number of conflicts remains at a much lower level than at the end of the Cold War'.[5] Moreover, say the authors, 'the recent decline in armed conflict after the end of the Cold War has now brought the probability of a country being in conflict to a level corresponding to the end of the 1950s and lower than at any later time during the Cold War'.[6] The Uppsala research goes farther than the others mentioned here, by adding data back to 1946. It concludes that there was 'a fairly steep decline [in conflict] throughout the first years of the Cold War and the de-Stalinization period, then a long, slow increase during the greater part of the Cold War, and finally another steep decline after the turbulence in certain parts of Eastern Europe at the end of the Cold War'.[7] Again, this bears out the hypothesis that the world nowadays is more, not less, stable than it was before the collapse of communism.

Final confirmation comes with the *Peace and Conflict Report* published by the Center for International Development and Conflict Management (CIDCM) at the University of Maryland. Published in 2003, this states, among other things, that:

- 'The decline in the global magnitude of armed conflict, which began in the early 1990s, has continued'.

- 'Ethnonational wars for independence, which were the main threat to civil peace and regional security in the first post-Cold War decade, have declined to their lowest level since 1960'.

- 'International crises declined in number and intensity throughout the 1990s'.[8]

The authors of the report state that:

> The global trend in major armed conflict has continued to decrease markedly in the post-Cold War era both in numbers of states affected by major armed conflicts and in general magnitude. According to our calculations, the general magnitude of global warfare has

---

[5] Nils Peter Gleditsch et al., 'Armed Conflict 1946-2001: A New Dataset', *Peace Research*, vol. 39, no. 5, 2002, p. 616.

[6] Ibid., p. 621.

[7] Ibid., p. 622.

[8] Monty G. Marshall & Ted Robert Gurr, *Peace and Conflict 2003* (College Park, MD: CIDCM, 2003), pp. 1-2.

decreased by over fifty percent since peaking in the mid-1980s, falling by the end of 2002 to its lowest level since the early 1960s.

This is strikingly illustrated in the following chart (adapted from the chart on page three of the CIDCM report above – for an explanation of 'magnitude', see footnote 8 below):[9]

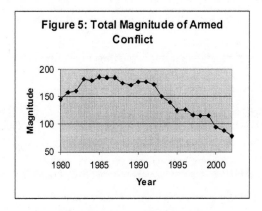

decreased by over fifty percent since peaking in the mid-1980s, fall-

The 'New Wars' Thesis

In response to this evidence that the world has not in fact become less stable since 1990, a common response is that the nature of conflicts has changed and they require a new type of response (namely more aggressive military intervention). This is the 'new wars' thesis. It is also based on an incorrect understanding of the facts. It is true that in most recent conflicts civilians, not soldiers, have been the main victims, and it is true that there have been some notorious atrocities. However, as Edward Newman states in a review of the academic literature on the subject, 'much of this is not new: all of the factors that characterize new wars have been present, to varying degrees, throughout the last 100 years. ... The difference today is that academics, policy analysts, and politicians are focusing on these factors more than before. ...

---

[9]　In this chart, 'The magnitude of each major armed conflict is evaluated according to its comprehensive effects on the state or states directly affected by the warfare, including numbers of combatants and casualties, size of the affected area and dislocated populations, and extent of infrastructure damage. It is then assigned a single score on a ten-point scale measuring the magnitude of its adverse effects on the affected society'. Marshall & Gurr, op. cit., p. 12, footnote 1.

Shifts in the causes, nature, and impact of war are more apparent than real'.[10] There is, as Newman concludes from his review, 'little evidence' to substantiate the claim that the human impact of 'new' wars, in terms of patterns of atrocity, human displacement and so forth, is worse than before.[11]

The Declining Incidence of Terrorism

Terrorism had also been declining since the mid-1980s until America and its allies embarked upon the 'War on Terror' in the early 2000s. This can be clearly seen on the following chart, drawn from the Memorial Institute for the Prevention of Terrorism's Knowledge Base Incident Analysis Wizard.[12] The chart displays international terrorist incidents between 1968 and 2004 (domestic terrorism is excluded as pre-1997 data was not collected):

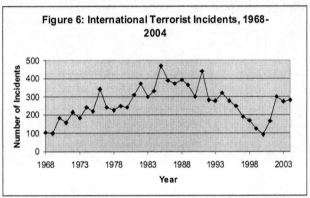

Figure 6: International Terrorist Incidents, 1968-2004

This shows a peak in terrorist activity in the mid-1980s, followed by a steady decline until a new upsurge began in 2001, although even now terrorists do not appear to be as active as in the 1980s. Another dataset, ITERATE, (*International Terrorism: Attributes of Terrorist Events*) confirms this trend, although it places the peak of terrorist activity in the late rather than mid-1980s.[13]

[10] Newman, op cit., p. 179.
[11] Newman, op. cit., p. 181.
[12] Available online at: www.tkb.org/ChartModule.jsp.
[13] Figures 6 & 7 are drawn from data published in Table 1 in Todd Sandler and Walter Enders, 'An Economic Perspective on Transnational

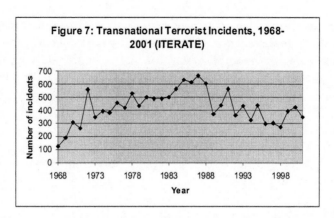

Figure 7: Transnational Terrorist Incidents, 1968-2001 (ITERATE)

At this point in the argument, doom-mongers often riposte with the claim that it may be true that the incidence of terrorism is going down but that this is compensated for by attacks becoming more deadly. If one excludes the attacks of 11 September 2001, however, this is also incorrect. According to the ITERATE statistics, terrorist-related deaths actually peaked between the mid-1970s and mid-1980s, and despite blips in 1998 and 2001 have generally been lower since:

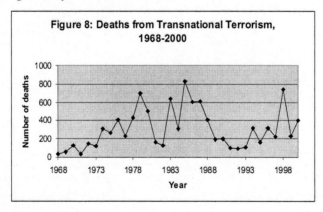

Figure 8: Deaths from Transnational Terrorism, 1968-2000

One can observe the same downwards trend in the US State Department's annual reports on *Patterns of Global Terrorism*, at least until 2003, in which year the State Department reported the

Terrorism', *The University of Alabama Economic, Finance and Legal Studies Working Paper Series*, Working Paper No. 03-04-02. Available online via www.cha.ua.edu.

first increase in terrorist activity for several years (after initially issuing a report claiming the opposite, a report which was subsequently withdrawn). Secretary of State Condoleeza Rice has now announced that the *Patterns of Global Terrorism* will no longer be published in its previous form. The reason appears to be embarrassment at an enormous rise in terrorist activity reported in 2004 – up from 175 incidents counted in 2003 to around 650 in 2004. These figures do not, as it happens, suggest that the West is under greater threat of attack, for of the 600 incidents 300 were in Kashmir and 200 in Iraq.[14] But, like the statistics above, they suggest that the incidence of terrorism was steadily going down until the United States launched its 'War on Terror', and that it has since risen again, most especially since the invasion of Iraq. In terms of counter-terrorism, the Iraq expedition has turned out to be a spectacular own-goal.

Conclusion

The data above makes it very clear that the hypothesis that the world became more dangerous and unstable after the collapse of communism is untrue. On the contrary, the end of the Cold War was a blessing in terms of international security. The world is significantly more peaceful now than it was ten or twenty years ago.

---

[14]   Jonathan S. Landay, 'Data Shows Record Number of Terror Attacks in Iraq in 2004', *Knight Ridder*, 26 April 2005. Available online at: www.realcities.com/mld/krwashington/11495462.htm.

Weapons of Mass Destruction

The term 'weapons of mass destruction' (WMD) is generally used to refer to nuclear, biological, and chemical weapons. Currently, paranoia about WMD lies behind much of the policy of expeditionary warfare. Doom-laden prognoses of future catastrophe at the hands of 'rogue states' or terrorists wielding WMD are used to justify 'preventive' wars of aggression, which are meant to forestall such catastrophes. As Chapter 2 pointed out, much of the hype about WMD exaggerates their potential. Indeed, the very term 'weapons of mass destruction' is a misleading one because it suggests that biological and chemical weapons are in some way both as destructive as nuclear weapons and worse than conventional armaments. Neither suggestion is true. This appendix provides some additional evidence to support this assertion.

Nuclear Weapons

Nuclear weapons undoubtedly are weapons of 'mass destruction'. The likelihood of such weapons being used against us by a 'rogue state' is, however, extremely low. Were Iran, for instance, to develop its own nuclear deterrent, it would certainly use it for precisely that purpose – as a deterrent. There could be no possible motive for it to launch an unprovoked nuclear attack on the United Kingdom or its allies (especially given the certainty of overpowering retaliation). Furthermore, at present Iran, North Korea and other potential nuclear powers lack the means to deliver weapons as far as the UK, and are unlikely to acquire such means in the foreseeable future. Finally, one must also bear in mind the fact that many commentators believe that the spread of nuclear weapons can enhance international stability, as it appears to have done in the instance of India and Pakistan, ensuring that future conflicts over Kashmir do not again turn into all-out war. There is perhaps less to fear from nuclear proliferation than the hysteria suggests.

Even if one rejects this argument, one can still argue that there are better ways of controlling proliferation than aggressive military action, which is only likely to encourage the potential targets of our aggression to develop their own deterrent as rapidly as possible. A first step might well be for the Western nuclear powers to do more to fulfil their binding obligations under the Non-Proliferation Treaty to reduce and eventually eliminate their own nuclear arsenals. At present, our example does not encourage others to remain nuclear-free.

Most observers accept that a nuclear attack on the UK by another state is exceptionally unlikely, but still justify military intervention against 'proliferators' on the grounds that these states might give any nuclear weapons they develop to terrorists. Here we run into the argument about the 'nexus of rogue states, terrorists, and weapons of mass destruction'.

The development of nuclear weapons requires a huge industrial infrastructure and so is beyond the means of any terrorist group. Any terrorist wishing to use such weapons would have to be given them ready-made by a state. Yet nobody has ever suggested any reason why a state would wish to make such a bizarre donation, especially a 'rogue state'. Countries like Iraq under Saddam Hussein, Iran, and North Korea, have very limited resources. Developing a nuclear weapon would be the culmination of a major national project. The resulting bomb or bombs would represent a national treasure of enormous value. Why on earth would they immediately give it away to uncontrollable fanatics? Their 'nukes' would be their firmest assurance that they would be safe from external attack, their ultimate deterrent against 'regime change'. Allowing terrorists to have their bomb would on the contrary be the surest way to provoke an attack against themselves.

In the end, therefore, the 'nexus' argument comes down to an assumption that leaders of 'rogue states' are insane, an assumption for which there is no evidence.

Given this, the terrorist nuclear threat actually boils down to 'dirty' or 'radiological' bombs. These are often portrayed in the press as potentially capable of causing 'mass destruction', leading to thousands, even tens of thousands, of deaths. The principle of a radiological bomb is that some radioactive material is dispersed using a conventional explosion. The number of people killed from the initial explosion would be no more than from any such attack (in other words, probably only a very few, if any). The 'mass' threat is more to those who might die prematurely (perhaps over many years) through exposure to radiation. Destruction of property would be very limited.

Opinions vary as to how many might suffer in this event. Some suggest that the numbers might be very great. However, according to Dr Theodore Rockwell, an expert on radiation interviewed for the BBC documentary *The Power of Nightmares*, 'I don't think it would kill anybody. You'll have trouble finding a serious report that would claim otherwise'. A simulation of a dirty bomb explosion carried out by the American Department of Energy, 'calculated that the most exposed individual would get a fairly high dose [of radiation], not life-threatening'. 'Even this minor threat is open to question', reported *The Guardian*, 'The test assumed that no one fled the explosion for one year'!![1]

In truth, the main purpose and effect of a dirty bomb would not be to cause 'mass destruction' but to cause mass panic as well as a huge clean-up bill for decontamination. Thus Dr Brian Jones, formerly the chief WMD expert of the British Defence Intelligence Staff, concludes that, 'Some would call a radiological weapon or "dirty bomb" a weapon of mass destruction, pre-

---

[1]   Andy Beckett, 'The Making of the Terror Myth', *The Guardian*, 15 October 2004.

sumably because it is vaguely "nuclear", but this is an exaggeration of its potential'.[2]

Biological Weapons

Biological weapons include both biological agents (bacteria, viruses and other organisms) and toxins derived from biological sources, such as ricin. They are easier to produce than nuclear weapons, and this makes them a much more realistic terrorist weapon. However, dissemination is problematic. One cannot simply put biological weapons in a bomb – the explosion will kill them. But large volumes of the agent or toxin would be needed to spread disease through a water system (and even then counter-measures could rapidly be taken) and bioweapons spread through the air are extremely vulnerable to atmospheric conditions (sun, rain, wind, etc rapidly kill most bio-agents).

Although in theory a terrorist could infect large numbers of people with a bioweapon, in practice, this would be extremely difficult. The Aum Shinrikyo sect in Japan, for instance, attempted on several occasions to poison the population of crowded Tokyo with anthrax, but failed to injure even one person. To use anthrax to infect large numbers of people, one needs to aerosolize the spores, which requires sophisticated laboratory equipment and dissemination systems. The 'wet' form of the disease made by groups such as Aum Shinrikyo is not suitable for widespread dissemination. Futhermore, those infected by anthrax can easily be treated by common antibiotics.

In another case, following the conviction of Kamel Bourgass in London in April 2005, British newspapers hysterically printed banner headlines about his 'plot to poison Britain' with ricin. But ricin is not a weapon of mass destruction. The most famous example of ricin poisoning was that of Bulgarian dissident Georgi Markov, whom the Bulgarian secret services murdered by injecting ricin into his bloodstream with a specially adapted umbrella. It would clearly be easier for terrorists to kill en masse using magazine-fed pistols than trick umbrellas. Kamel

[2]   Brian Jones, *War, Words and WMD*. Available online at:
       www.sussex.ac.uk/Units/spru/hsp/17-11-03%20Jones%20Paper.pdf

Bourgass supposedly planned to 'poison Britain' by smearing ricin on car door handles. It is most unlikely that he would have killed anybody with this method. As one critic rightly notes, 'To use ricin to kill many people, someone would have to dump hundreds of tons of it on a small area. To kill many with anthrax or botox, someone would have to first get the victims to sniff weapons-grade anthrax or eat botulism-contaminated food and then shun antibiotics or antitoxins'.[3] These are not practical methods of causing mass destruction.

The only real way a terrorist could succeed with bioweapons would be to deliberately infect himself with a deadly disease such as smallpox and then seek to infect as many people as possible before succumbing to the disease himself. If the disease spread sufficiently rapidly, serious damage could theoretically result. There are problems even with this scenario, however. First, the terrorist would somehow have to overcome the considerable problem of getting hold of smallpox. Second, diseases such as smallpox spread fairly slowly, and as the SARS outbreak revealed, can be contained through methods such as quarantine in a such a way as to limit the number of deaths very substantially.

Chemical Weapons

Chemical weapons are the simplest to make of the trio of WMD, and also the least effective. They can be delivered as gases or vapours, or in liquid form. In the right conditions, especially in confined spaces, they can indeed kill very large numbers. However, in the open air, very large volumes of chemical agent are needed, and the chemicals are vulnerable to meteorological conditions. In a military context, protection is easily achieved through the use of respirators and chemical suits. As a result, during World War One it took on average one ton of gas to inflict one casualty. In wartime, the main purpose of chemical weapons would be to disrupt enemy activity by temporarily contaminating areas rather than to kill the enemy in large numbers.

---

[3] Alan Reynolds, 'WMD Doomsday Distractions', *The Washington Times*, 10 April 2005.

What this means is that a terrorist who used chemical weapons in a confined space, such as a theatre or an underground train, might have some success, but the numbers of dead would be limited to scores, or at worst hundreds of people (whom the terrorist could equally easily kill using conventional explosives or other weapons[4]). As Brian Jones concludes:

> To produce large numbers of casualties an appropriate concentration of the chemical has to be achieved over a wide area that contains a large number of potential victims, and despite the highly toxic nature of some chemicals, and the low concentrations needed, *very large quantities* of CW are required for this sort of military use. ... It is difficult to see even the most potent chemical agents (including toxins of biological origin) in the hands of terrorists as a threat to national security.[5]

Conclusion

Alan Reynolds of the Cato Institute in the USA notes that, 'The postwar death toll from bioterrorism is only six – five Americans from anthrax and one Bulgarian assassinated with ricin. The death toll from chemical terrorism is 26 – 19 from sarin gas in Japanese subways a decade ago and seven in Chicago in 1982 killed by Tylenol laced with cyanide'.[6] By contrast, in the Second World War, the various belligerents succeeded in killing 60 million people using various forms of bullet, bomb, and high explosive; in the most notorious example of mass murder of recent times, the 1994 genocide in Rwanda, one of the main instruments of death was the humble machete; and most recent large-scale terrorist atrocities (such as the Oklahoma, Bali, and Madrid bombings) were caused by high explosives (sometimes of a home-made variety). These statistics should give those who insist on categorising chemical and biological weapons as weapons of 'mass destruction' pause to think.

---

[4] In fact, when Aum Shinrikyo conducted a carefully planned attack using the nerve agent Sarin to murder commuters on the Tokyo underground in 1995, it managed to kill only a dozen people. A few years later a lone lunatic threw a Molotov cocktail onto an underground train in Seoul and succeeded in killing over 100.

[5] Jones, op. cit.

[6] Reynolds, op. cit.

What this shows is that if we are really in search of the main threat to contemporary security, it does not come from 'rogue states' and their WMD, but rather from terrorists using thoroughly traditional methods of destruction. We should not underestimate the capacity of such attacks to harm us, but we should also remember that it is very limited. Terrorists using bullets and bombs are not going to bring our civilisation to its knees. They do not pose, as Mr Blair and others have bizarrely suggested, an 'existential' threat. The scale of our response to them – billions of pounds of expenditure on an ever-increasing military capacity to engage in preventive military intervention overseas, as well as the use of this capacity in places such as Iraq – seems excessive in the extreme.

Intervention and Just War Theory

Chapter 3 raised philosophical objections to the current policy of military intervention and referred to Just War Theory in support of those objections, with particular reference to Thomas Aquinas. This appendix provides further information about the ethics of war in support of that argument.

Discussions of the ethics of war normally divide the matter into two: *jus ad bellum*, which concerns the rules determining when one is allowed to wage war; and *jus in bello*, which concerns what one is permitted to do during war. More recently some thinkers have also begun to speak of a third area, *jus post bellum* – the argument being that the justice of a war depends not only on why it was fought and how it was fought but also on what happens after it is over. For the purpose of this book, however, we are concerned solely with *jus ad bellum*, and specifically whether the rules of *jus ad bellum* justify the waging of aggressive wars of intervention to 'do good'.

Nearly every literate culture has devoted at least some attention to considering criteria for what makes a war 'just'.[1] With the possible exception of the Islamic world, the West has done so in the most systematic way, developing what is known as 'just war theory'. This has its origins in the teachings of the Catholic Church, with additions by secular philosophers from the

---

[1] The different approaches of the world's main cultures and religions on this issue are compared in my earlier book: Paul Robinson (ed.), *Just War in Comparative Perspective* (Aldershot: Ashgate, 2003).

Renaissance onwards (such as Hugo Grotius).[2] Just war theory is traditionally held to have begun with St Augustine, but Augustine's teachings on the ethics of violence are spread over many works and never consolidated. It was not until the *Summa Theologica* of Thomas Aquinas that a systematic theory developed with three criteria put together in one place. These are the ones used in Chapter 3. As mentioned there, these criteria have subsequently expanded, and although different authorities now sometimes give slightly different lists, most state that to be 'just', a war must meet the following conditions:[3]

- **Just cause**. Those waging the war may do so only for a just cause. Generally, this is interpreted as meaning only defence against aggression.
- **Right intention**. It is considered unjust to do the right thing with impure motives, for instance to fight an aggressor not out of a love of justice but for personal profit or hate. Impure intentions will eventually degrade the behaviour of those fighting for even the most just cause.
- **Legitimate authority.** Only those endowed with legitimate authority to wage war may do so.
- **Reasonable Chance of Success**. To wage war when one has no chance of winning is futile and wastes life. It is, therefore, unjust.
- **Last Resort**. One must have exhausted all other reasonable alternatives to obtain justice before one embarks on war.
- **Proportionality**. The harm done by the war must not be disproportionate to the goal for which the war is being fought.

[2]   It should be noted that although just war theory arose out of Catholic teaching, the modern Catholic Church is far from united in favour of it. Under Pope John Paul II and now Benedict XVI, the emphasis has turned more and more towards an ethic of peacemaking. This has had the effect of making war even harder to justify than it was already. Prior to becoming Pope in 2005, Cardinal Joseph Ratzinger made it clear that the principle of 'preventive war', and the US-led invasion of Iraq, did not correspond to Catholic teaching.

[3]   The most cited contemporary work on just war theory is Michael Walzer, *Just and Unjust Wars: A Moral Argument with Historical Illustrations*, 2nd ed. (New York: Basic Books, 1992). Also important are writers such as James Turner Johnson, Paul Ramsey, George Weigel, John Kelsay, and Brian Orend.

Not every contemporary philosopher accepts all of these criteria, but most of the arguments are not about the criteria *per se* but about how to interpret them. For instance, debates over humanitarian intervention often centre on whether intervention to prevent human rights abuses constitutes 'just cause' or whether the sole just cause is self-defence against aggression. Similarly, the United States claimed before the invasion of Iraq that, as a democratic state, it possessed legitimate authority to wage war. Most European states felt that because all United Nations members abjure to that organisation the right to initiate war, the only authority capable of legitimising military action was the UN Security Council. Thus even the UK justified its participation in the invasion by reference to long outdated UN Security Council Resolutions authorising the use of force to remove Iraqi forces from Kuwait in 1991.

Just war theory is imprecise (the criteria being open to various interpretations), and so frequently leaves room for both supporters and opponents of any given war to invoke elements of it in their cause. Given this, the key point is perhaps that all six criteria must be met for a war to be just. If even one condition is not met, the war is unjust. This places the hurdle extremely high, a fact which is not always appreciated. Consequently, it is not at all easy to make a good case justifying most of the wars fought by the United Kingdom since the end of the Cold War within the confines of just war theory.

Making intervention a keystone of defence policy requires one to turn a blind eye to centuries of ethical thinking purely on the grounds of expediency and power. There are so-called 'Realists' who believe that war lies outside the realm of moral philosophy, but those who do not include themselves in that category should pause before endorsing a doctrine which is so fraught with moral problems.

Counter-Terrorist and Counter-Insurgency Theory

It is a cliché that the greatest threat to British security in the early twenty-first century comes from terrorism. If we take this assumption for granted, one question which arises is whether the maintenance of large armed forces and a policy of interventionist expeditionary warfare are appropriate responses to the threat of terrorism. If not, we are clearly wasting national resources on a futile and possibly counter-productive strategy.

Chapter 4 argued the above case, with reference to British counter-terrorist doctrine. This appendix therefore outlines that doctrine in more detail.

Simply put, there are three ways in which a state can deal with a threat from terrorists (such as the IRA or Al-Qaeda) or insurgents (such as those fighting British and American occupation forces in Iraq):

- The state can treat the situation as a purely military affair, and seek to win by killing or capturing all the insurgents. This is known as the *War Model*. In cases where the insurgents have very limited popular support, this can succeed. The model does assume, however, that there are a finite number of insurgents/terrorists, whereas all too often the effect of the war model is to create new enemies every time some of them are eliminated. As a result, this approach is unlikely to succeed in situations where the insurgents or terrorist do have some popular appeal, unless it is accompanied by state terror of such great proportions that potential new recruits are frightened into submission.

- The state can defeat the insurgents/terrorists by isolating them from the civil population through the simple expedient of removing the civil population, either by driving it out of the countryside or by killing it off. For obvious reasons, this is not considered an acceptable tactic by contemporary Western democratic states.

- The state can defeat the insurgents/terrorists by isolating them from the civil population by more friendly methods. This is the basis of British counter-terrorist and counter-insurgency doctrine. According to British theory, a campaign against terrorists or insurgents can be seen as having three elements. On one side is the government, on the other side the terrorists/insurgents, and in the middle the mass of the population. Whoever controls the middle will eventually prevail. The terrorists will win if they can persuade the middle ground by propaganda or deeds or intimidation to support them or remain neutral. Similarly if the government can win the support of the terrorists' home base, it will acquire the intelligence it needs to identify the terrorists and eliminate them in a targeted and discriminate fashion. There is a role for military force in this third option, but it is a limited one. Ultimately success rests on the development and implementation of a political strategy and on the use of good intelligence and selectively applied force.

This British counter-terrorist doctrine is often said to originate in the Malayan Emergency of 1948-1960, in which the British successfully defeated a communist insurgency. The British experience in Malaya is often contrasted with the failure of the Americans in Vietnam, although differences between the two conflicts make such comparisons problematic.

The lessons from Malaya were summarised by Robert Thompson, who was an administrator in the country during the Emergency. In his book, *Defeating Communist Insurgency*,

Thompson listed five principles of counter-insurgency doctrine:[1]

- *'The government must have a clear political aim*: to establish and maintain a free, independent and united country, which is politically and economically stable and viable'. According to Thompson, 'an insurgent movement is a war for the people'. A high priority must be given to establishing a sound administration and maintaining or restoring law and order.

- *'The government must function in accordance with the law'.* If it does not, it cannot expect the population to. Tough laws are permissible, but they must be properly applied. The government must be seen to follow legal procedure. This way it wins the respect of the target population.

- *'The government must have an overall plan,* covering not just security measures and military operations, but all political, social, economic, administrative, police and other measures which have a bearing on the insurgency'.

- *'The government must give priority to defeating the political subversion, not the guerrillas'.* This isolates them from the civil population and so allows their destruction.

- 'In the guerrilla phase of an insurgency, *the government must secure its base areas first'.*

What is noticeable about Thompson's principles is that four of them are essentially political and only one is military. This reflects the belief that insurgency is a political problem which must be dealt with primarily by political methods. Military action which undermines the political effort, however successful it may be, cannot be condoned.

Thompson's ideas were developed further by General Sir Frank Kitson, who fought for the British Army during the Mau-Mau insurgency in Kenya. Kitson determined that the key to success in fighting insurgents and/or terrorists was the gathering and collating of intelligence about them. Adding Kitson to

[1]   Robert Thompson, *Defeating Communist Insurgency: Experiences from Malaya and Vietnam* (London: Chatto & Windus, 1966), pp. 50-8.

Thompson, the British Army has created six principles of counter-terrorism. These principles are as follows:

- Recognition of the political nature of the problem, and, accordingly, the solution.
- Civilian supremacy, command, and control.
- Information/intelligence.
- Splitting the insurgent/terrorist from the people by:
  - Propaganda
  - Hearts and minds
  - Physical barriers
- Destroying the isolated insurgent/terrorist.
- Political reform to prevent recurrence.

It is clear that the military interventionism practised by the British armed forces as part of the American-led 'Global War on Terror' contradicts these principles: military activity has taken priority over political strategy; there is no obvious 'overall plan' or even political aim; and too often Anglo-American forces have acted in a way which in the eyes of many contradicts the principles of international law. It is unsurprising that our focus on a military response to terrorism has so far proved less than successful.

In the light of all this, the usefulness of the mass of the British armed forces as a response to terrorism must be brought into question. Aircraft carriers, tanks, heavy artillery, submarines, fighter aircraft, sophisticated radar systems, and the like, have almost no role in combating small groups of individuals who live hidden in urban populations. A carefully-considered political strategy, combined with patient police work and intelligence gathering, is far more likely to pay dividends in terms of defending the British people against the terrorist threat.

Force Planning Models

Chapter 6 drew attention to force planning models and the flaws in the current vogue for 'capabilities-based planning'. It suggested that this represented upside-down defence planning. This appendix analyses force planning in more depth. It should be apparent from what follows that defence policy is rarely the direct product of goal-oriented logic. Rather the outputs of policy are a muddled product of a series of compromises between different external pressures. The fact that this is inevitably the case does not mean that we should be satisfied with this state of affairs and admit the impossibility of creating a rational planning model. Instead, it imposes a burden on us to try to reduce the inconsistencies as much as possible, and do all we can to bring the existing model in line with the theoretical ideal. We will never succeed in reaching that ideal, but we can at least reject practices which diverge wildly from it. Current defence planning is such a practice.

British strategist Colin Gray has identified three conceptual lenses through which one can observe defence planning:[1]

- **The Rational Actor Model.** In this model, policy is the goal-directed activity of a single agent. The government chooses its defence and security objectives, and defence and security policy is then devised directly to secure those objectives.

[1]   See Colin S. Gray, *Canadian Defence Priorities* (Toronto: Clarke, Irwin & Co, 1972).

- **The Organisational Process Model.** In this model, policy is the product of a complex bureaucratic organisation that approaches problems in a particular way. One might say that the policy is a result not so much of rational pursuit of goals as of the structure and nature of the organisation which produces it.

- **The Government (or Bureaucratic) Politics Model.** In this model, policy is the product of a process of bargaining between men and women occupying positions of authority in various organisations. Defence policy in this instance would be not a plan designed to attain certain objectives but the result of conflict and compromise between, for instance, the Ministry of Defence and other departments as well as the Treasury, and between various actors within the Ministry of Defence (e.g. inter-service rivalries), among others.

Another way of looking at defence planning is to focus on the approach used by the planners themselves. In an article in *Fundamentals of Force Planning*, Henry C. Bartlett identified eight such approaches:[2]

- **Top Down**. According to Bartlett, 'Objectives drive the *Top Down* force planning approach. The first step is to determine what the decision maker wants to accomplish. The second is to develop a strategy or game plan which specifies how the objective or objectives will be achieved. ... Forces to implement the strategy are then determined'.

- **Bottom Up.** Here one bases one's plans on whatever capabilities one already possesses. New capabilities cannot be created quickly (it takes up to 20 years to develop a major new piece of military hardware), and so there is sense in doing shorter-term planning on the basis of what one can do, as opposed to what one would like to do. This approach is less useful, though, for long-term planning.

- **Scenario**. In this approach 'force planning is situationally driven'. The planner imagines scenarios in which the mili-

---

[2]   Henry C. Bartlett, 'Approaches to Force Planning', in *Fundamentals of Force Planning*, vol. 1, Chapter 3.C.1 (Newport, RI: Naval War College Press, 1990), pp. 443-453.

tary might need to operate, and then devises force structures to operate in those scenarios.

- **Threat**. 'The *Threat* emphasis is driven by opponent capability'. The planner first quantifies that capability and then creates the forces which would be needed to defeat it should war ever break out with that opponent.

- **Mission**. This is 'functionally driven. The force planner starts with broad categories of wartime mission activities', and creates the forces required to carry these out.

- **Hedging**. Here the planner is not certain what the threat is, what scenarios he might be operating in, or what missions his forces might have to carry out. He therefore hedges his bets and tries to cover as many eventualities as possible. This provides some security in times of uncertainty but may lead to worst-case planning and excess capacity.

- **Technology**. Here technology drives policy. Planners create capabilities to a large degree because technology allows them to.

- **Fiscal**. This is budget-driven planning. Overall defence spending is set by factors which are not related to defence needs (e.g the strength of the economy, the demands of other departments, and so forth). Planners have to make the best of what is available.

In practice, defence policy mixes all of these approaches. The ideal model shown in Chapter 6 can be seen as a form of the Rational Actor Model incorporating both Top Down and Threat-based planning. It seeks to create military forces to defend against threats and to pursue military objectives in a rational fashion. This is what one would hope defence policy would be about. The Bureaucratic Politics Model probably resembles more closely what happens in reality, but it is not a model one would ever recommend.

Furthermore, one must note that with the exception of the Bottom Up approach, all the approaches listed by Bartlett are designed to work towards a determination of military capabilities. Capabilities are the end of the planning process, not the start. Capabilities-based planning is a mockery of rational decision-making. It is not surprising, therefore, that it did not exist before the end of the Cold War and that it does not exist in Bartlett's list (published in 1990). Its sudden appearance in the 1990s when all the other approaches dictated massive cuts in military expenditure indicates that it is not a logical method of planning but rather a bureaucratic mechanism to justify continued spending.

World Defence Spending

The following chart gives figures for world defence spending in 2003 in millions of US dollars, as well as statistics on numbers of personnel in both regular and reserve armed forces. All figures are drawn from the International Institute for Strategic Studies' *Military Balance 2004-2005*. Since 2003, both NATO and the EU have expanded their membership considerably. For continuity, this table lists only those members of NATO who were part of the organisation in 2003.

Figure 9: World Defence Spending

Country	Defence Spending (US$m)	Regular Personnel	Reserve Personnel
Global Total	**997,158**	**20,358,400**	**32,967,300**
USA	404,920	1,427,000	1,237,700
UK	42,782	212,600	272,500
Other NATO			
Belgium	3,923	40,800	13,700
Canada	10,118	52,300	36,900
Czech Republic	1,871	57,000	n/a
Denmark	3,334	22,800	64,900
France	45,695	259,000	100,000
Germany	35,145	284,500	358,600
Greece	7,169	177,600	291,000

Hungary	1,589	33,400	90,300
Iceland	n/a	n/a	n/a
Italy	27,751	200,00	63,200
Luxembourg	233	900	n/a
Netherlands	8,256	53,100	32,200
Norway	4,387	26,600	219,000
Poland	4.095	163,000	234,000
Portugal	3,173	44,900	210,900
Spain	9,944	150,700	328,500
Turkey	11,649	514,800	378,700
Total NATO	**626,033**	**3,721,000**	**3,932,190**
Non-NATO Europe	30,148	991,500	4,599,200
Russia	65,200	960,600	2,400,000
China	55,948	2,250,000	550,000
East Asia & Australasia	108,431	4,407,100	15,173,900
Central & South Asia	24,388	2,509,500	1,347,500
Middle East & North Africa	54,148	2,885,600	2,560,700
Caribbean, Central & South America	25,145	1,300,100	2,123,900
Sub-Saharan Africa	7,716	1,333,000	280,000

NATO's 2003 defence expenditure of $626,033 million accounts for 62.8% of the entire world's defence spending of $997,158 million. Given the recent increases in US defence spending and the addition of new members to NATO, this percentage must now be even higher.

Also, if one adds together the spending in 2003 of the 25 nations which now make up the EU, one finds that it amounts to $208,185 million. This means that the EU spends on defence almost double the amount spent by China and Russia combined ($121,148 million). What these statistics reveal is that any security problems which Europe or the Western World in general face are not the product of either low defence spending or a lack of military personnel or equipment. Our military power is overwhelming and more than sufficient to cope with any possible future threat.

The Precautionary Principle

In terms of government policy making, the phrase 'precautionary principle' is one most closely associated with environmental protection. In this regard, it refers to something somewhat different to the concept I have used in Chapter 8. Nonetheless, an analysis of the environmental precautionary principle does shed some light on the validity of 'just in case' defence planning as well as on the principle of preventive war.

The precautionary principle entered European environmental thinking from the German *Vorsorgeprinzip*, a concept used by post-war Federal German governments to take preventive action, introduce new regulations, and seize control of environmental policy from the länder. As Sonja Boehmer-Christiansen notes, prior to *Vorsorgeprinzip*, 'the prevailing free market philosophy discouraged regulation, most of which remained in the hands of the länder or communes'. From this it is clear that the drive for precaution is in part related to power, and its consequence is increased government activity.[1] In terms of military affairs, therefore, we must conclude that those supporting the principle are likely to be driven by power considerations, and that its implementation is likely to lead to increased military activity.

---

[1] Sonja Boehmer-Christiansen, 'The Precautionary Principle in Germany – Enabling Government', in Tim O'Riordan and James Cameron (eds), *Interpreting the Precautionary Principle* (London: Earthscan, 1994), pp. 31-60.

In environmental terms, the principle is defined in the following way:

> Where there are threats of serious or irreversible damage, lack of full scientific certainty shall not be used as a reason for postponing cost-effective measures to prevent environmental degradation.[2]

Thus, according to David Freestone and Ellen Hey, 'the essence of the precautionary concept, the precautionary principle, is that once a risk has been identified the lack of scientific proof of cause and effect shall not be used for not taking action to protect the environment'.[3]

This has a number of implications. First, it implies taking anticipatory or preventive action to prevent future harm. Second, it involves a reversal of the burden of proof – it is not government's responsibility to prove that a certain activity is harmful before prohibiting it, it is the responsibility of the alleged purveyor of harm to prove that his actions are not harmful.

If we apply this principle to matters of security, we see that it can be used to justify actions such as the invasion of Iraq – the potential of future harm from Iraqi WMD and links with terrorists required preventive action, and the burden of proof was shifted onto Iraq to prove that it had no WMD and taken off Britain and the USA to prove that it did.

However, the principle can simply be reversed. In environmental cases, as often as not it is used to prevent people doing possibly harmful things (overfishing, polluting, etc). This means that it should be more applicable to stopping people engaging in war than allowing them to do so. Since we know that historically wars have done more harm than good, caution, far from permitting preventive war, would seem to suggest that the burden of proof must be shifted to those wishing to start wars to prove that their actions are beneficial.

---

[2]   David Freestone and Ellen Hey, 'Origins and Development of the Precautionary Principle', in David Freestone and Ellen Hey (eds), *The Precautionary Principle and International Law* (Kluwer Law International, 1996), p. 3.

[3]   Ibid, p. 13.

Likewise, if we consider whether it is wise to invest money in defence 'just to be safe', we must consider the known costs of acting in such a way, and the precautionary principle can then be used to say that we should not spend money on defence unless we can prove that doing so will not bring us harm.

At any rate, what these examples show is that the precautionary principle is one that can be used both ways – to take action as a precaution against something, or to caution against acting. This shows that as a basic planning principle it suffers from a grave weakness.

This is not the only problem associated with the concept. As one critic notes, 'the precautionary principle is too vague to serve as a regulatory standard because it does not specify how much caution should be taken'.[4] This leads to the difficulty cited in Chapter 7, namely that if one is going to spend money 'just in case' there is no obvious reason why one has chosen a particular quantity of money and not two, three, or four times as much, or any other multiple. Decisions become entirely arbitrary. To be fair to environmentalists, they do say that preventive measures should be taken only when there are 'reasonable grounds for concern' even if those grounds are not proven.[5] But that is far removed from justifying defence spending on a 'just in case' basis, for in that instance there are no 'reasonable grounds', merely a desire to cover every conceivable angle.

This leads to another problem, which is that in reversing the burden of proof the precautionary principle allows people to act in contravention of the prevailing evidence. As Bill Durodie, Director of the International Centre for Security Analysis, Kings College London, told the BBC programme *The Power of Nightmares*:

> In essence, the precautionary principle says that not having the evidence that something might be a problem is not a reason for not taking action as if it were a problem. That's a very famous triple-negative phrase that effectively says that action without evidence is justified. It requires imagining what the worst might be and applying that imagination upon the worst evidence that currently exists.

---

[4] D. Bodansky, cited in Boehmer-Christiansen, op. cit., p. 52.
[5] Freestone and Hey, op. cit., p. 6.

... Once you start imagining what could happen, then – then there's no limit. What if they had access to it? What if they could effectively deploy it? What if we weren't prepared? What it is is a shift from the scientific, 'what is' evidence-based decision making to this speculative, imaginary, 'what if'-based, worst case scenario.[6]

Finally, it must be remembered that there are opportunity costs associated with precaution. The resources spent on environmental protection, defence, and so forth, to secure us against unknown and unproven dangers, are resources which are no longer available to be used against known and proven dangers. The consequence may be that caution does more harm than good.

Put together, what this analysis suggests is that precaution by itself is not a sound basis for policy making. This has important implications both for the concept of preventive war which is so important in contemporary defence policy and for the idea of 'just in case' defence spending. It suggests that the arguments in favour of both ideas are considerably weaker than their supporters maintain.

---

[6]   *The Power of Nightmares*, BBC TV, 3 November 2004.

Bibliography

Abramowitz, Morton, 'Does Iraq Matter?', *The National Interest*, Spring 2004.

Aquinas, Thomas, *Summa Theologica* (New York: Benziger Brothers, 1947).

Boehmer-Christiansen, Sonja, 'The Precautionary Principle in Germany – Enabling Government', in Tim O'Riordan and James Cameron (eds), *Interpreting the Precautionary Principle* (London: Earthscan, 1994), pp. 31-60.

Booth, Ken, 'Ten Flaws of Just Wars', in Ken Booth (ed.), *The Kosovo Tragedy: The Human Rights Dimensions* (London: Frank Cass, 2001).

Buzan, Barry, *People, States and Fear: An Agenda for International Security in the Post-Cold War World* (London: Harvester Wheatsheaf, 1991).

Chandler, David, 'Rhetoric without Responsibility: The Attraction of "Ethical" Foreign Policy', *British Journal of Politics and International Relations*, vol. 5, no. 3, August 2005.

Chopra, Jarat, 'The Obsolescence of Intervention Under International Law', in Marianne Heiburg (ed.), *Subduing Sovereignty: Sovereignty and the Right to Intervene* (London, 1994).

Clausewitz, Karl von, *On War*, ed. Anatol Rapaport (London: Penguin, 1982).

Cooper, Robert, *The Breaking of Nations: Order and Chaos in the Twenty-First Century* (London: Atlantic, 2003).

Cooper, Robert, 'Imperial Liberalism', *The National Interest*, no. 79, Spring 2005.

Dyer, Gwynne, *War* (New York: Stoddart, 1985).

Freestone, David, & Hey, Ellen, 'Origins and Development of the Precautionary Principle', in David Freestone and Ellen Hey (eds), *The Precautionary Principle and International Law* (Kluwer Law International, 1996).

Fundamentals of Force Planning, vol. 1 (Newport, RI: Naval War College Press, 1990).

Garden, Timothy, & Ramsbotham, David, 'About Face: The British Armed Forces – Which Way to Turn?', *RUSI Journal*, April 2004.

Gleditsch, Nils Peter, et al., 'Armed Conflict 1946-2001: A New Dataset', *Peace Research*, vol. 39, no. 5, 2002.

Kaldor, Mary, 'Humanitarian Intervention: a Forum', *Nation*, vol. 270, no. 18, 8 May 2000, pp. 21-5.

Kagan, Robert, *Paradise and Power: America and Europe in the New World Order* (London: Atlantic, 2003).

International Institute for Strategic Studies, *The Military Balance, 2004-2005* (Oxford: OUP, 2005).

Marshall, Monty G., & Gurr, Ted Robert, *Peace and Conflict 2003* (College Park, MD: CIDCM, 2003).

Ministry of Defence, *Delivering Security in a Changing World*, Defence White Paper, December 2003 (London: The Stationery Office, 2003).

Ministry of Defence, *Delivering Security in a Changing World: Future Capabilities*, Defence Command Paper Cm 6269, July 2004 (London: The Stationery Office, 2004).

Ministry of Defence, *The Strategic Defence Review* (London: The Stationery Office, 1998).

Ministry of Defence, *The Strategic Defence Review: A New Chapter* (London: The Stationery Office, 2002).

Morris, Julian, *Rethinking Risk and the Precautionary Principle* (London: Institute of Economic Affairs, 2000).

Moseley, Alexander, & Norman, Richard (eds.), *Human Rights and Military Intervention* (Aldershot: Ashgate, 2002).

Newman, Edward, 'The "New Wars" Debate: A Historical Perspective is Needed', *Security Dialogue*, vol. 35, no. 2, June 2004.

Nye, Joseph, *Bound to Lead: The Changing Nature of American Power* (New York: Basic Books, 1990).

Nye, Joseph, *Soft Power: The Means to Succeed in World Politics* (New York: Public Affairs, 2004).

Priest, Dana, & Hsu, Spencer, 'U.S. Sees Drop in Terrorist Threats', *Washington Post*, 1 May 2005.

Project Ploughshares, 'Introduction', *Armed Conflicts Report 2004*. Available online at: www.ploughshares.ca/content/ACR/ACR00/ACR04-Introduction.html

Robinson, Paul, *Just War in Comparative Perspective* (Aldershot: Ashgate, 2003).

Sadowski, Y., 'Ethnic Conflict', *Foreign Policy*, no. 111, Summer 1998, pp. 12-23.

Sandler, Todd, & Enders, Walter, 'An Economic Perspective on Transnational Terrorism', *The University of Alabama Economic, Finance and Legal Studies Working Paper Series*, Working Paper No. 03-04-02. Available online via http://www.cha.ua.edu

SIPRI Yearbook 2004: Armaments, Disarmament and International Security (Oxford: OUP, 2004).

Smith, Dan, Trends and Causes of Armed Conflict, Berghof Research Center for Constructive Conflict Management, available online via www.berghof-handbook.net

Thompson, Robert, *Defeating Communist Insurgency: Experiences from Malaya and Vietnam* (London: Chatto & Windus, 1967).

Walzer, Michael, *Just and Unjust Wars: A Moral Argument with Historical Illustrations*, 2nd ed. (New York: Basic Books, 1992).

SOCIETAS: essays in political and cultural criticism

Public debate has been impoverished by two competing trends. On the one hand the trivialization of the media means that in-depth commentary has given way to the soundbite. On the other hand the explosion of knowledge has increased specialization, and academic discourse is no longer comprehensible. As a result writing on politics and culture is either superficial or baffling.

This was not always so — especially for politics. The high point of the English political pamphlet was the seventeenth century, when a number of small printer-publishers responded to the political ferment of the age with an outpouring of widely-accessible pamphlets and tracts. Indeed Imprint Academic publishes facsimile C17th. reprints under the banner 'The Rota'.

In recent years the tradition of the political pamphlet has declined—with most publishers rejecting anything under 100,000 words. The result is that many a good idea ends up drowning in a sea of verbosity. However the digital press makes it possible to re-create a more exciting age of publishing. *Societas* authors are all experts in their own field, but the essays are for a general audience. Each book can be read in an evening. The books are available retail at the price of £8.95/$17.90 each, or on bi-monthly subscription for only £5/$10. Details: **imprint-academic.com/societas**

EDITORIAL ADVISORY BOARD

IMPRINT ACADEMIC, PO Box 200, Exeter, EX5 5YX, UK
Tel: (0)1392 841600   Fax: (0)1392 841478   sandra@imprint.co.uk
imprint-academic.com/societas